# THE PUZZLE OMNIBUS

# THE PUZZLE OMNIBUS

## Gyles Brandreth

TREASURE PRESS

*Publisher's Note: Nearly all the puzzles in this book appear in both imperial and metric measurements. However, occasionally only one set of measurements is given.*

First published in Great Britain in 1987 by
William Collins Sons & Co Ltd

This edition published in Great Britain in 1990 by
Treasure Press
Michelin House
81 Fulham Road
London SW3 6RB

Designed by Clive Sutherland

ISBN 1 85051 380 5

Printed in Yugoslavia

# CONTENTS

# ACKNOWLEDGEMENTS

Grateful acknowledgement is made to the following for kind permission to reproduce copyright material: for Puzzles 233 and 234, The First Crossword and The Second Crossword, *The St Louis Post Dispatch*; for Puzzle 235, A D-Day Crossword, the *Daily Telegraph*; for Puzzles 239, 240 and 241, Printer's Devilry, Give And Take and Next-Door Neighbours, Victorama Ltd; for Puzzle 242, Murder Mystery, Stephen Sondheim and *New York Magazine*; for Puzzle 243, Sir Max Beerbohm's Crossword, *Times* Newspapers (News International).

# INTRODUCTION

Do you know the story of a journalist called John Rhee who worked on *Life* magazine in New York in the early 1950s? He was a delightful chap by all accounts, amiable, even-tempered, level-headed, and, above all, *reliable*. So when he didn't turn up for work one fine Spring morning his colleagues were surprised. When he failed to show up the next day and calls to his apartment went unanswered, his colleagues became alarmed. On the third day they hired a private detective to help find the missing journalist. The detective spent a week on the assignment, searching high and low, visiting all John Rhee's known haunts, questioning every one of his friends, his colleagues, his contacts. In every area he drew a blank. And then at the end of the seventh day, and towards the end of his tether, the frustrated detective called in at a bar on the lower East Side and there he saw him, the missing scribe, sitting at a side table nursing a mid-life crisis and a Scotch on the rocks. Relief mingled with triumph as the detective approached the journalist and declared, 'Ah, sweet Mr Rhee of *Life*, at last I've found you!'

Well, dear reader, I've not yet unravelled the mystery of life. Where are we going? Why are we here? What's it all about? I don't know. Do you? Let's face it: life's a puzzle. But my philosophy is that while we may not know the destination we might at least enjoy the journey. Even if we can't all resolve the riddle of existence, there are other puzzles – some of them almost as challenging – that are not utterly beyond our ken. This is a book for those, like me, who while wrestling with the enigma of existence want to relax with brain-teasers of a slightly simpler sort.

*The Puzzle Omnibus* aims to be a comprehensive collection of mental challenges of all kinds. It runs from the ancient world to the late twentieth century, from Archimedes, an arch-puzzler in his day, to a modern master like Michael Curl. If you're a puzzle nut like me you'll be gratified to discover as you travel through the book that we're in excellent company. With riddles Queen Victoria *was* amused. Max Beerbohm concocted the world's only unsolvable crossword. Lewis Carroll had more fun in puzzledom than in Wonderland.

Abraham Lincoln was an adept puzzler. His favourite was this conundrum: 'If the tail of a dog was called a leg, how many legs would a dog have?' Think about it for a moment, then curse the shade of honest Abe as he gives you his answer: 'Four – calling a tail a leg doesn't mean that it is one!'

Ninety-nine per cent of the answers to the puzzles in this book are rather more straightforward than that. I have given the puzzles a star-rating – one star for the easiest, five for the most fiendish – but what's a nightmare for one may be a doddle for another. When I was asked to think of the only day of the week that can be turned into another word it took me seven hours' hard labour – truly – to eliminate Tuesday to Sunday. Monday is the day, but what's the anagram? If you know the answer it's easy, but if you don't it isn't so obvious. Ponder for a moment, then glance at the foot of the page and kick yourself.

Come to think of it, kicking oneself is an occupational hazard for puzzlers. It's part of the pleasure. They do say we're MASH STOICS, don't they?

Gyles Brandreth.

MONDAY = DYNAMO

# 1.

# CHILD'S PLAY

Here, to begin with, is a selection of easy traditional puzzles – puzzles that have intrigued and entertained generation after generation of schoolchildren.

## 1
## UP AND DOWN *

This is a very old riddle: What is it that you can put up a chimney down but that you cannot put down a chimney up?

## 2
## THE FROG *

A frog is at the bottom of a 30-foot well. Each hour he climbs three feet and slips back two feet. How many hours does it take him to get out?

## 3
## INDIANS *

Two Indians sat in their wigwam. The shorter one was the taller one's son, but the taller one was not the shorter one's father. How was this possible?

## 4
## A CHEMICAL COMPOUND *

Which common chemical compound is represented by these letters?

H  I  J  K  L  M  N  O

## 5
## AN ANAGRAM ★

Can you rearrange the following eleven letters to make just one word:

D E J N O O R S T U W

## 6
## SOCKS ★

In a drawer I have five pairs of grey socks and five pairs of blue socks. In the dark, what is the smallest number of single socks I would have to take out to be sure of getting a matching pair?

## 7
## A STRANGE HOUSE ★

The windows on all four sides of my house face north. How do you think that is possible?

## 8
## A PUZZLING RHYME ★

Can you make sense of this puzzling rhyme?

Y Y U R

Y Y U B

I C U R

Y Y 4 ME

## 9
## CIGARETTE ENDS ★

A tramp makes his own cigarettes out of cigarette ends that he collects. Seven ends will make one cigarette. If he has collected forty-nine ends how many cigarettes will he be able to make from them?

## 10
## WHICH IS HEAVIER? ★

Which is heavier: a pound (kilogram) of feathers or a pound (kilogram) of lead?

## 11
## HOW MANY ANIMALS? ★

A farmer was asked how many animals he had. He replied 'They're all horses but two, all sheep but two, and all pigs but two.'
    How many animals did the farmer have?

## 12
## AN ALARMING PUZZLE ★

Last night I went to sleep at 9 p.m., having previously wound up and set my alarm clock to wake me at 10 a.m. I slept soundly until the alarm clock woke me. How many hours' sleep did I get? (NB: this puzzle won't work if you use a digital alarm clock.)

## 13
## ODD BOOKS ★

Here are the titles of five famous books, but each word in the titles has been scrambled. Can you unscramble the words and reveal the correct titles?

(a)  RIVOLE TWITS            (d)  THEIRPAWS WOND

(b)  HET MITE CHEMINA        (e)  TELLIT MENOW

(c)  NONORIBS SOURCE

## 14
## HOW OLD IS HOWARD? ★

When Howard is twice as old as he is now, he will be three times as old as he was three years ago.

How old is Howard now?

## 15
## A QUESTION FOR COOKS ★

If potatoes should be boiled for twenty minutes, can you say how long sausages should be grilled?

## 16
## FIVE-LETTER ANIMALS ★

Here are five 5-letter names of animals. Take one letter from each name in turn to spell out the 5-letter name of another animal.

Z  E  B  R  A

T  A  P  I  R

S  H  E  E  P

H  O  R  S  E

P  A  N  D  A

## 17
## GEORGE AND MILDRED ★

George and Mildred have seven daughters. Each of the daughters has a brother. How many are there in the family, including George and Mildred?

## 18
## AGES ★

Algernon is older than Basil but younger than Cyril, who is older than Dinsdale, who is older than Algernon.

Who is the oldest and who is the youngest?

## 19
## EGG TIMERS ★

For his breakfast Mr Shell likes an egg that has been boiled for exactly two minutes. He has two egg timers: one that runs for three minutes and one that runs for five minutes.

How can he use these egg timers to make sure that his egg is cooked just the way he likes it?

## 20
## FAMOUS SHIPS ★

On the left are the names of five famous ships, each one associated with an equally famous person or group of people. Can you sort out the list on the right, and get the correct people to their ships.

| | |
|---|---|
| Endeavour | Francis Drake |
| Golden Hind | Lord Nelson |
| Mayflower | Christopher Columbus |
| Santa Maria | The Pilgrim Fathers |
| Victory | Captain Cook |

## 21
## IT'S ALL RELATIVE ★

Who is my father's only child's daughter's brother?

## 22
## WHICH IS GREATER? ★

Which is greater – six dozen dozen or half a dozen dozen?

## 23
## COUNTRY NAMES

If you look closely at some names of countries, you will find that they contain boys' or girls' names. For example, MARK is contained in DENMARK. Now try these:

(a) Find a boy's name in SUDAN.

(b) Find a girl's name in CANADA.

(c) Find a boy's name in the PHILIPPINES.

(d) Find a girl's name in AMERICA.

(e) Find a boy's name in INDONESIA.

(f) Find a girl's name in ARGENTINA.

(g) Find a boy's name in NEW ZEALAND.

(h) Find a boy's name in AUSTRALIA.

(i) Find a girl's name in GREAT BRITAIN.

(j) Find a boy's name in HUNGARY.

## 24
## TWO COINS

I have two coins, totalling 55 pence. One of the coins is not a 50 p piece. What are the two coins?

## 25
## SPOTTY DOGS

The total number of spots on two spotty dogs is ninety-six. If one spotty dog has eighteen more spots than the other spotty dog, how many spots are there on each of the spotty dogs?

## 26
## FIVE-LETTER BIRDS

Here are five 5-letter names of birds. Take one letter from each name in turn to spell out the 5-letter name of another bird.

R O B I N

E A G L E

D I V E R

H E R O N

S N I P E

## 27
## DON AND CARL ★

At eight o'clock Don sets out from Doncaster to Carlisle, driving his car at a steady fifty miles per hour (eighty kilometres per hour). An hour later, Carl sets out from Carlisle to Doncaster, driving his car at a steady sixty miles per hour (one hundred kilometres per hour).

When the two cars pass each other, which is nearer to Doncaster?

## 28
## A FIRST-CLASS PUZZLE ★

Class 1A were given tests in history and geography. Three-quarters of the pupils got full marks in the history test and three-quarters got full marks in the geography test.

If every pupil got full marks in at least one test, how many got full marks in both tests?

## 29
## SANDWICH FILLING ★

Replace the asterisks by the name of something you may have in a sandwich. Do so correctly and nine 3-letter words will appear when you read downwards.

```
I   S   T   E   L   S   F   O   T

*   *   *   *   *   *   *   *   *

P   W   Y   U   D   Y   N   E   N
```

## 30
## CONSECUTIVE ODD NUMBERS ★

Three consecutive odd numbers are multiplied together, giving the result 1287. What are the three numbers?

## 31
## MISSING GIRLS ★

Complete each word by replacing the asterisks with a girl's name of three letters.

(a)  ***OUNCE

(b)  CL***RLY

(c)  REIS***

(d)  B***ZARD

(e)  BIG***

(f)  ***PERED

(g)  PR***ILING

(h)  ***MANT

## 32
## SAVINGS ★

A boy had been saving 5p and 20p coins in his piggy-bank. When he emptied the piggy-bank he found it contained forty-four coins totalling exactly £4.

How many coins of each kind did the piggy-bank contain?

## 33
## SPELLING TEST ★

Of the ten words below, six are spelt correctly and four are spelt incorrectly. Which are the four incorrect words and how should they be spelt?

|     |           |     |           |
|-----|-----------|-----|-----------|
| (a) | AERIAL    | (f) | EIGHTH    |
| (b) | PARALEL   | (g) | PNEUMONIA |
| (c) | WIERDNESS | (h) | DAFFODIL  |
| (d) | CONCEITED | (i) | COMITTEE  |
| (e) | SEPERATE  | (j) | RHYTHM    |

## 34
## GRANDFATHER AND GRANDSON ★

A grandfather is forty-four years older than his grandson. Five years ago he was five times as old as his grandson.

How old are the grandfather and grandson now?

## 35
## LITTER CHANCE ★

I'm sorry, the title of this puzzle should have been LETTER CHANGE.

What you have to do is change only one letter in each word to make a sensible phrase from each of the lines below.

|     |                   |     |                  |
|-----|-------------------|-----|------------------|
| (a) | ODD RATHER TAME   | (e) | HONEY FOX HAM    |
| (b) | PET RICE QUACK    | (f) | LOST BUN GOT FEAST |
| (c) | NIGHT END MAID    | (g) | LANCE FUR JOB    |
| (d) | JELLY FOOD YELLOW | (h) | WIND LOOSE CHASM |

## 36
## WHAT'S THE SPORT? ★

In which sport do the winners move backwards and the losers move forwards?

## 37
## A PIECE OF CAKE

If a cake is cut into six equal pieces, each piece would be 1½ ounces (40 grammes) heavier than if the cake were to be cut into eight equal pieces.

What is the weight of the cake?

## 38
## BOOMERANG BALL

An Australian Aborigine can throw a boomerang so that it comes back to him without hitting any obstruction. How can you do the same trick with an ordinary tennis ball?

## 39
## A TALE OF FOUR CITIES

There are four cities in Ruritania. Alphaville is due north from Betaville. Gammaville is due east from Alphaville. Deltaville is due south from Gammaville.

Which city is due east from Betaville?

## 40
## FIVE-LETTER COUNTRIES

Here are five 5-letter names of countries. Take one letter from each name in turn to spell out the 5-letter name of another country.

M A L T A

S P A I N

B U R M A

I T A L Y

S U D A N

## 41
## RACING RESULTS

Five girls took part in a race. Alison finished before Bunty but behind Clare. Debby finished before Emma but behind Bunty.

What was the order in which they finished the race?

## 42
## FRUIT

If I buy a melon and a coconut, the cost will be £1.19. If I buy a melon and a pineapple the cost will be £1.45. If I buy a coconut and a pineapple the cost will be £1.40.

What is the price of each fruit individually?

## 43
## WORK IT OUT ★

Add 6 to a certain number and then divide by 10. The result is the same as it would be if you had subtracted 4 and divided by 8.
    What is the number?

## 44
## MISSING BOYS ★

Complete each word by replacing the asterisks with a boy's name of three letters.

(a) ***PARD            (e) ROAD***E

(b) CUS***ER           (f) H***WAY

(c) DEST***ER          (g) DEF***CE

(d) CHIC***            (h) IDE***ST

## 45
## BUYING SWEETS ★

A woman went into a sweetshop to buy some sweets. She spent one-third of the money she had with her and then spent another 30 pence, leaving herself with exactly three pounds.
    How much money did she spend?

## 46
## WHAT'S MY LINE? ★

Here are the names of ten jobs that have become rather mixed up. For example, the first one should be BAKER. Can you sort out the others?

(a) BREAK               (f) VERY SOUR

(b) THE CURB            (g) NO STAMP

(c) THE RACE            (h) MENIAL COP

(d) THE MICS            (i) CARRY TEES

(e) GO NURSE            (j) EAT IN CIRCLE

---

### Quizzical Quote

'To ask the hard question is simple.'

*W. H. Auden*

---

## 47
## FIVE-LETTER CAPITALS ★

Here are five 5-letter names of capital cities in Africa. Take one letter from each name in turn to spell out the 5-letter name of another capital city in Africa.

A C C R A

R A B A T

T U N I S

D A K A R

L A G O S

## 48
## ROUND THE CLOCK ★★

In the twelve-hour period from noon to midnight how many times does the minute hand of a clock pass the hour hand?

## 49
## AIRLINES ★★

To which countries do these airlines belong?

(a) AER LINGUS

(b) KLM

(c) QANTAS

(d) PAN-AM

(e) EL AL

(f) AEROFLOT

(g) LUFTHANSA

(h) SABENA

## 50
## NOUGHTS AND CROSSES ★★

I am sure that everyone reading this book knows the game of Noughts and Crosses (which, in America, is also known as Tic-Tac-Toe), so I need not bother describing it.

   Between two expert players, every game will end in the same result. Either the first player should always win, the second player should always win, or every game should be drawn. Which is correct?

---

**Quizzical Quote**

'Man is a puzzle-solving animal.'

*R. A. Knox*

---

# FILM STARS ★★

Can you sort out the names of these twelve film stars? Half the letters in their names have been replaced by stars!

  (a)  J*H* W*Y*E

  (b)  H*M*H*E* B*G*R*

  (c)  J*L*E *N*R*W*

  (d)  S*L*E*T*R *T*L*O*E

  (e)  B*R*R* S*R*I*A*D

  (f)  S*E*E *C*U*E*

  (g)  G*E*D* J*C*S*N

  (h)  P*U* N*W*A*

  (i)  H*Y*E* M*L*S

  (j)  M*R*O* B*A*D*

  (k)  R*B*R* M*T*H*M

  (l)  G*L*I* H*W*

# FIND THE NUMBER ★★

Five-sixths of a certain number is seven less than eight-ninths of the same number. Find the number.

# SPORTING PLACES ★★

What game or sport is associated with each of these places in Great Britain?

  (a)  Wimbledon          (e)  Twickenham

  (b)  The Oval           (f)  Isle of Man

  (c)  St Andrews         (g)  Cowes

  (d)  Epsom              (h)  Bisley

## COMPLETE THE COUNTRIES ★★

Here are the names of six countries with the vowels left out. When complete, all the names contain the same number of letters.

Can you add the vowels to complete each country's name?

(a) STR    (d) MRCC

(b) LGR    (e) LBN

(c) LBR    (f) LBNN

---

### Twenty Tantalizing Tongue-Twisters

Try saying each of these tongue-twisters ten times, quickly.

Red lorry, yellow lorry.
Cuthbert's custard.
Knapsack strap.
Truly rural.
Lame lambs limp.
Six thick thistles.
Cheap ship trips.
Lemon liniment.
Critical cricket critics.
Throw three free throws.
Sister Suzie sews a sheet.
Around the rugged rocks the ragged rascal ran.
Is there a pleasant peasant present?
Three thrice-freed thieves.
She sells seashells by the seashore.
The Leith police dismisseth us.
That bloke's back brake-block broke.
The sixth sheik's sixth sheep's sick.
Thirty thousand feathers on a thrush's throat.
Which wristwatches are Swiss wristwatches?

---

# 2.

---

# NUMBER PUZZLES

---

### 55
### TOM, DICK AND HARRY ★

Tom, Dick and Harry have a sum of $575 to be divided between them. They agree to divide it so that Tom receives $19 more than Dick, and Dick receives $17 more than Harry.

How much does each man receive?

### 56
### DIGGORY'S HOLE ★

Diggory, who is 6 feet (1.8 metres) tall, is standing in a hole that he has started digging. He plans to carry on digging until the depth of the hole is twice his own height – and then, he calculates, the top of his head will be three times as far below the ground as it is now above the ground.

How deep is the hole now?

### 57
### LEFT-HANDED TEAPOTS ★

On Sunday a market trader acquired a bargain lot of left-handed teapots (only slightly cracked) which he was able to sell very cheaply. On Monday he sold half a teapot more than half the teapots he had bought. On Tuesday he sold half a teapot more than half the remainder. On Wednesday he sold half a teapot more than half what was left. He then had one teapot left, which he sold on Thursday.

How many teapots did he sell altogether?

## 58
## ON THE STREET WHERE I LIVE ★

On the street where I live there are six adjoining houses, built in the last century, with house numbers running consecutively in even numbers. The sum of the six numbers is 666.

What is the highest of the six numbers?

## 59
## A BRIDGE PROBLEM ★

A river which is 580 feet (177 metres) wide is spanned by a bridge which has one-sixth of its length on the east bank and one-seventh of its length on the west bank.

How long is the bridge?

## 60
## POTATOES ★★

A farmer has three piles of potatoes. For every six potatoes in the first pile there are seven potatoes in the second pile, and for every eight potatoes in the second pile there are nine potatoes in the third pile.

If there are 3674 potatoes altogether, how many are there in each pile?

## 61
## EUSTACE AND HILDA ★★

Hilda is twice as old as Eustace used to be when Hilda was as old as Eustace is now.

If Eustace is now twenty-one, how old is Hilda?

## 62
## A TRIP TO THE SEASIDE ★★

A coach operator organized a trip to the seaside. The prices were £3.25 for adults and £1.70 for children. He sold fifty tickets for a total amount of £128.40.

How many children's tickets did he sell?

## 63
## BOOK CHOICE ★★

I asked Professor Sinewave to show me some of his textbooks. He showed me eight books on arithmetic, ten books on geometry, and twelve books on algebra. He kindly offered to let me borrow any two of the books – provided that they were not both on the same subject.

In how many different ways could I choose which two books to borrow?

## 64
## JACK AND JILL ★★

Jack and Jill go up the hill at a speed of 1½ miles per hour (2.4 kilometres per hour), and they come down at a speed of 4½ miles per hour (7 kilometres per hour). If it takes them exactly 2 hours to make the double journey, how far is it from the bottom of the hill to the top?

## 65
## ON THE BUSES ★★

If you reverse the digits in the age of Mr Bus you get the age of Mrs Bus. Mr Bus is older than Mrs Bus and the difference between their ages is one-eleventh of the sum of their ages.

How old are Mr and Mrs Bus?

## 66
## A FOWL QUESTION ★★

If a hen and a half will lay an egg and a half in a day and a half, how many eggs would six hens lay at the same rate in six days?

## 67
## MULTIPLES OF SEVEN ★★

The sum of seven consecutive multiples of seven is 1960. What are the seven numbers?

## 68
## YOUNG ROTHSCHILD ★★

Young Rothschild saved 5p, 20p and 50p coins in his piggy-bank. One day he opened it to find out how much he had saved. He found that he had a total of £7, and that he had three more 20p coins than 50p coins, and three times as many 5p coins as 20p coins.

How many coins of each denomination did he have?

## 69
## THE WIDOW'S LEGACY ★★

A gentleman who recently died left the sum of $300,000 to be divided among his widow, four sons and five daughters. In his will he directed that each son should receive twice as much as each daughter, and that each daughter should receive three times as much as their mother.

How much did the widow receive?

## 70
## LONGFELLOW'S BEES ★★

When the poet Henry Wadsworth Longfellow was Professor of Modern Languages at Harvard, he used to amuse himself by setting unusual arithmetic puzzles for his students. Here is one of Longfellow's puzzles.

If one-fifth of a hive of bees flew to the ladamba flower, one-third flew to the slandbara, three times the difference between these two numbers flew to an arbor, and one bee continued to fly about, attracted on each side by the fragrant ketaki and the malati, what was the number of bees?

## 71
## WINE AND WATER ★★

I fill a wine-glass half full of wine and another glass twice the size one-third full of wine. Then I top up each glass with water and empty the contents of both glasses into a tumbler.

Now, how much of the mixture is wine and how much is water?

## 72
## CRICKET SCORES ★★

In a cricket match Archer made fifty-six runs. Baxter scored twice as many as Clifford and three times as many as Dexter, but Archer's score exceeded Baxter's by the same number of runs that Clifford's exceeded Dexter's.

Can you give the correct score of each man?

## 73
## SHARE DEALING ★★

Monty withdrew two-thirds of the money that he had in his bank account to buy some shares. A week later he sold the shares at a loss, receiving only two-thirds of the price that he had paid for them. When he paid this money into his bank account, he found that as a result of his unsuccessful share dealing he now had £500 less in his account than he had originally.

How much did he have in his account originally?

## 74
## UPSTREAM, DOWNSTREAM ★★

'The steamer,' remarked Captain Fishfinger, 'was able to go twenty miles an hour (thirty-two kilometres an hour) downstream, but could only do fifteen miles an hour (twenty-four kilometres an hour) upstream. So, of course, she took five hours longer in coming upstream from A to B than in going downstream from B to A.'

What is the distance between A and B?

## 75
## REMAINDERS ★★

Can you find a number, under 3000, which when divided by 2 leaves a remainder of 1; divided by 3, a remainder of 2; divided by 4, a remainder of 3; divided by 5, a remainder of 4; divided by 6, a remainder of 5; divided by 7, a remainder of 6; divided by 8, a remainder of 7; divided by 9, a remainder of 8; divided by 10, a remainder of 9?

## 76
## MILES AND MINUTES ★★

A travels at the rate of $x$ miles an hour, while B travels at the rate of $x$ minutes a mile. Obviously, if $x$ is 30, then A is much faster; while if $x$ is 3, then B is much faster.

What must the value of $x$ be, for A and B to be travelling at the same speed?

## 77
## THE UNIVERSAL FRIENDLY SOCIETY ★★★

Have you heard about the Universal Friendly Society? Its aims are to encourage people to be friendly to everyone they meet.

The society holds a meeting once a month, and it is the invariable rule for every member present to shake hands once with every other member present.

At the first meeting, there were fifteen members present. How many handshakes were there at this meeting?

At the second meeting, there were exactly twice as many handshakes as at the first meeting. How many members were present at the second meeting?

# CRYPTARITHMETIC

In Cryptarithmetic the solver is presented with the form of an arithmetic operation – addition, subtraction, multiplication or division – but with letters of the alphabet (or other symbols) replacing the digits, each letter standing for a different digit. The solver has to work out which digit is represented by each letter and thus restore the original calculation.

No one knows for sure when this sort of puzzle originated, although it seems that it was quite well-known in India and China at least a thousand years ago.

The term Cryptarithmetic was originated in 1931 by a Monsieur Vatriquant writing under the pseudonym Minos in *Sphinx*, a Belgian magazine of recreational mathematics. A cryptarithmetic puzzle is often called a cryptarithm.

In 1955 the puzzle creator J. A. H. Hunter coined a new word – Alphametic – to describe a cryptarithm in which the letters used form meaningful words.

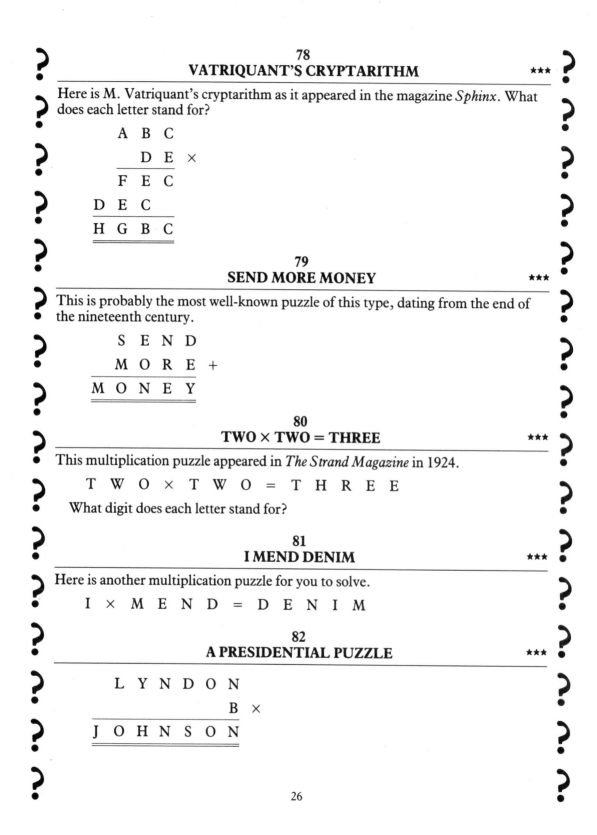

## 78
### VATRIQUANT'S CRYPTARITHM ★★★

Here is M. Vatriquant's cryptarithm as it appeared in the magazine *Sphinx*. What does each letter stand for?

```
    A  B  C
       D  E  ×
    ─────────
    F  E  C
 D  E  C
 ────────────
 H  G  B  C
```

## 79
### SEND MORE MONEY ★★★

This is probably the most well-known puzzle of this type, dating from the end of the nineteenth century.

```
    S  E  N  D
    M  O  R  E  +
 ───────────────
 M  O  N  E  Y
```

## 80
### TWO × TWO = THREE ★★★

This multiplication puzzle appeared in *The Strand Magazine* in 1924.

T  W  O  ×  T  W  O  =  T  H  R  E  E

What digit does each letter stand for?

## 81
### I MEND DENIM ★★★

Here is another multiplication puzzle for you to solve.

I  ×  M  E  N  D  =  D  E  N  I  M

## 82
### A PRESIDENTIAL PUZZLE ★★★

```
 L  Y  N  D  O  N
             B  ×
 ────────────────
 J  O  H  N  S  O  N
```

## A NEW DEAL PUZZLE   ★★★

This puzzle was published in America at the time of President F. D. Roosevelt and the New Deal.

$$U \ S \ A \ + \ F \ D \ R \ = \ N \ R \ A$$

$$U \ S \ A \ + \ N \ R \ A \ = \ T \ A \ X$$

What digit does each letter represent?

## FLY FOR YOUR LIFE   ★★★

```
    F  L  Y
    F  O  R
 Y  O  U  R  +
 L  I  F  E
```

Can you decode this addition, given that I = 1 and O = 0?

## SCRABBLE   ★★★

```
    L  E  T  T  E  R  S
 A  L  P  H  A  B  E  T  +
 S  C  R  A  B  B  L  E
```

---

**Quizzical Quote**

'Amusement is one of the fields of applied mathematics.'

*W. F. White*

---

## 86
## THE SOLITARY SEVEN

****

Can you reconstruct this long division in which only one digit is given? There is a unique solution.

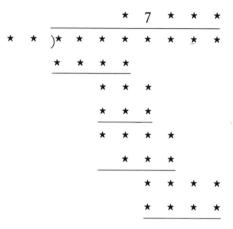

When this puzzle was first published in *The Strand Magazine*, the following clues were given: 'As the divisor when multiplied by 7 produces only three figures we know that the first figure in the divisor must be 1. We can then prove that the first figure in the dividend must be 1; that, in consequence of bringing down together the last two figures of the dividend, the last but one figure in the quotient must be 0, that the first and last figures in the quotient must be greater than 7, because they each produce four figures in the sum, and so on.' That should be sufficient to get you started.

## 87
## THE SIX NOUGHTS

***

| | | A. | | | | B. | | | | C. | | |
|---|---|---|---|---|---|---|---|---|---|---|---|---|
| | | 1 | 1 | 1 | | 1 | 1 | 1 | | 1 | 0 | 0 |
| | | 3 | 3 | 3 | | 3 | 3 | 3 | | 0 | 0 | 0 |
| | | 5 | 5 | 5 | | 5 | 0 | 0 | | 0 | 0 | 5 |
| | | 7 | 7 | 7 | | 0 | 7 | 7 | | 0 | 0 | 7 |
| | | 9 | 9 | 9 | | 0 | 9 | 0 | | 9 | 9 | 9 |
| | 2 | 7 | 7 | 5 | 1 | 1 | 1 | 1 | 1 | 1 | 1 | 1 |

Write down the little addition sum A, which totals 2775. Now substitute six noughts for six of the digits so that the sum shall be 1111. In the example B, five noughts have been substituted, and in example C nine. Can you do it with six?

## 88
## GRANT'S SON AND GRANDSON                                    ★★★

The combined ages of Grant and his son total 100 years. When Grant's son is as old as Grant is now, Grant's son will be five times as old as Grant's grandson is now. By then, however, Grant's grandson will be eight years older than Grant's son is now.

How old is Grant's grandson now?

## 89
## THE RAJAH'S DIAMONDS                                        ★★★

An Indian Rajah died, leaving a certain number of valuable diamonds. He left his first son one diamond and one-seventh of the remainder; his second son two diamonds and one-seventh of what then remained; his third son then received three diamonds and one-seventh of the diamonds left over, and so on, the last son receiving as many diamonds as there were sons and one-seventh of the remainder. Thus all the diamonds were disposed of.

How many sons were there, and how many diamonds?

## 90
## ROOTS                                                       ★★★

Which is larger: the tenth root of 10 or the cube root of 2?

## 91
## FAIR SHARES                                                 ★★★

Two travellers sat down to a frugal repast. One produced five loaves and the other three. Then a stranger came upon the scene and asked permission to eat with them. He produced no bread himself, but the three shared the eight loaves equally. Then the stranger put down eight cents in payment of his share.

How should the money be divided fairly between the two travellers?

## 92
## REGISTRATIONS                                               ★★★

The current system of vehicle registrations in some countries is based on a registration number consisting of a letter for the year, followed by three digits, followed by a three-letter combination. In fact, some three-letter combinations are never used because they form rude or embarrassing words.

If all three-letter combinations could be used, what would be the maximum number of vehicles that could be registered in one year, using this system?

By what number is the theoretical maximum reduced for each embarrassing three-letter combination that does not get used?

## 93
## SHARING A BICYCLE ★★★

Sturmey and Archer have to go 20 miles (32 kilometres) and arrive at exactly the same time. They have only one bicycle. Sturmey can walk only 4 miles an hour (6½ kilometres an hour) while Archer can walk 5 miles an hour (8 kilometres an hour), but Sturmey can ride 10 miles an hour (16 kilometres an hour) to Archer's 8 miles an hour (13 kilometres an hour).

How are they to arrange the journey, one leaving the bicycle on the road for the other to pick up? Each man always either walks or rides at the speeds mentioned, without any rests.

## 94
## DIVIDING THE CORN ★★★

A man rented a farm and contracted to give his landlord two-fifths of the produce. However, before the time came round for the division of the corn the tenant used 45 sackfuls. When the general division was made, it was proposed to give the landlord 18 sackfuls from the heap as his share of the 45 which the tenant had used, and then begin to divide the remainder as though none had been taken.

Would this method have been correct? If not, why not?

## 95
## THE WEIGHING-MACHINE FRAUD ★★★

Five children thought of a scheme to weigh themselves on an automatic machine at the cost of a single coin. Two of them got on the stand at the same time, and one of them changed places with another until all the ten possible pairs had been weighed. The results (in pounds and kilogrammes) were as follows: 114 (51.7), 115 (52), 118 (53.5), 119 (54), 121 (55), 122 (55.3), 123 (55.8), 125 (56.7), 126 (57) and 129 (58.5).

What were the individual weights of the five children?

## 96
## NON-PRIMES ★★★

Can you find one thousand consecutive integers which are not primes?

---

### Quizzical Quote

'Brain: an apparatus with which we think that we think.'

*Ambrose Bierce*

---

## BETELGEUSIAN MATHEMATICS ★★★

Yesterday I had a visitor from Betelgeuse (that's the third on the left past the Crab Nebula). After he had shown me round his flying saucer and given me a quick trip round the solar system, we started talking about life on Betelgeuse and how it differed from Earth.

Among the things he told me was that Betelgeusian mathematics is not quite the same as ours. As an example, he showed me some calculations he had been making, which are perfectly correct according to Betelgeusian mathematics:

$$5 \times 5 = 34$$

$$12 \times 12 = 144$$

$$16 \times 16 = 331$$

To see whether I understood, he asked me to tell him the Betelgeusian square root of 1552. I could not work it out. Can you?

## PRIME FACTORS ★★★

How many numbers less than 200 can be expressed as the product of three different prime factors? (1 is not to be considered a prime factor.)

## CONFUSING DATES ★★★

The firm that I work for has offices in Europe and in the USA. I get memos sent to me by Europeans and by Americans. The problem is that I sometimes get confused when I try to work out when a memo was written.

As you are probably aware, Americans do not write the date the same way that we do in Britain (and in Europe, generally). In Europe, when we write a date in figures, we write it in the order: day, month, year. To us a date of 7.4.87 means April 7th. But Americans write the date as: month, day, year – so for an American 7.4.87 is July 4th.

Therefore, when I see a date like 7.4.87, I have to check whether the writer is American or European before I can be sure what it means. Of course, some dates are unambiguous. 22.1.87 can only mean January 22nd (written by a European) and 5.15.87 can only mean May 15th (written by an American).

My question is: what percentage of the days in the year are ambiguous because of confusion between these two ways of writing the date?

## 100
## THE NEW STUDENTS ★★★

It was the start of a new academic year, and I was in Professor Sinewave's office looking at the lists of new students.

'Have you noticed something remarkable about the total number of new students?' Professor Sinewave said to me. 'It's a very interesting number. It can be expressed as the sum of three different 3-digit numbers, each of which when divided by 3 leaves a remainder of 1, when divided by 5 leaves a remainder of 2, when divided by 7 leaves a remainder of 3, and when divided by 9 leaves a remainder of 4.'

'Obviously,' I lied. 'I was just about to comment on that remarkable fact, myself.'

What was the number of new students?

## 101
## THE SOOPER MICROCOMPUTER ★★★★

The new Sooper Microcomputer is only available by mail order and has only been on sale for the past two weeks. The sales manager told me today that the value of orders received in the first week was $223,427. In the second week the value of orders was $363,593.

Given that the price of a Sooper Microcomputer is a whole number of dollars with no odd cents, perhaps you can work out the price you would have to pay for one.

## 102
## ROOT EXTRACTION ★★★★

In a conversation I had recently with Professor Sinewave, I had occasion to refer to the extraction of cube roots. 'Ah,' said the Professor, 'it is astonishing what ignorance prevails on that elementary matter! The world seems to have made little advance in the process of extracting roots since the primitive method of employing spades, forks and trowels for the purpose. For example, nobody but myself has ever discovered the simple fact that, to extract the cube root of a number, all you have to do is to add together the digits. Thus, ignoring the obvious case of the number 1, if we want the cube root of 512, add the digits – 8, and there you are!'

I suggested that this was a special case. 'Not at all,' he replied. 'Take another number at random – 4913 – and the digits add up to 17, which is the cube root of 4913.'

I did not presume to argue the point with the learned professor, but I will just ask the reader to discover all the other numbers whose cube root is the same as the sum of their digits. They are so few that they can be counted on the fingers of one hand.

The number 111,111 is exactly divisible without remainder by 3, 7 and 13 and therefore also by 21, 39, 91 and 273. It is also divisible by 1, by 11, by 111 and by 111,111 itself. In fact, altogether there are thirty-two integers which will divide into 111,111 without remainder.

What is the sum of these thirty-two integers?

## 104
### NO REPEATS

★★★★

Here is what looks like a very simple problem. How many positive integers are there in which no digit occurs more than once?

---

### Archimedes' Cattle Problem

This little gem of a puzzle is attributed to Archimedes. It is certainly very ancient – and no one has yet provided a solution!

The puzzle concerns a number of cattle, divided into four herds – white, black, dappled and yellow. The number of bulls is greater than the number of cows. We are given the following facts to work on:

1 The number of white bulls is ½ + ⅓ of the number of black bulls plus yellow bulls.
2 The number of black bulls is ¼ plus ⅕ of the number of dappled plus yellow bulls.
3 The number of dappled bulls is ⅙ plus ⅐ of the number of white plus yellow bulls.
4 The number of white cows is ⅓ plus ¼ of the number in the black herd.
5 The number of black cows is ¼ plus ⅕ of the number in the dappled herd.
6 The number of dappled cows is ⅕ plus ⅙ of the number in the yellow herd.
7 The number of yellow cows is ⅙ plus ⅐ of the number in the white herd.
8 The number of white and black bulls is a square number.
9 The number of dappled and yellow bulls is a triangular number.

Find the number of cattle of each type.

If you think you might be able to work this out on your pocket calculator or home computer, I will just give you a word of warning. In 1860 one mathematician estimated the number of cattle involved to be 766 times 10 to the power of 206,542. If this number was written out it would be half a mile (one kilometre) long!

## 105
## DIGITAL MULTIPLICATION ★★★★

Arrange the nine digits (excluding zero) to form three numbers so that the first number is the product of the other two. Here is one way:

$$5796 = 483 \times 12$$

Note that each of the nine digits appears once and once only. How many different ways can you find of doing this? The numbers you form may contain from one to four digits.

## 106
## CATS AND MICE ★★★★★

A number of cats killed 1,111,111 mice, every cat being responsible for an equal number of mice.

As there were more mice killed by each cat than there were cats, it is interesting to discover just how many cats there were in all.

## 107
## TELEPHONE NUMBERS ★★★★★

It was 4 a.m. when the telephone rang by my bedside. In a dazed state, I groped for the receiver. Before I had a chance to say anything, I heard a breathless, excited voice that I recognized instantly.

'Hello, my dear friend. This is Professor Sinewave here. I hope I have not disturbed you. I just had to call to tell you about an incredible fact I have discovered about your telephone number and mine. They are, as you know, both six-digit numbers. Well, the square of your number is exactly one greater than twice the square of mine. Isn't that amazing?'

'It certainly is,' I agreed. 'But 4 a.m. is really not the best time to give me a call about squares! Goodnight, Professor.'

I put down the phone, but it was a couple of hours before I was able to get back to sleep.

I hope that you won't have a sleepless night when you try to work out, from the Professor's information, what our two telephone numbers are.

---

### Quizzical Quote

'There is nothing so unthinkable as thought, unless it be the entire absence of thought.'

*Samuel Butler*

---

# SAM LOYD

Sam Loyd (1841–1911) was America's greatest creator of puzzles. His first chess problem was published in the *New York Saturday Courier* when he was fourteen, and he was soon recognized as the country's leading composer of chess problems. Until about 1870 he edited and contributed to chess columns in a variety of newspapers and magazines.

During the 1870s he turned his attention to mathematical puzzles. He also devised many novelty advertising give-aways, demonstrating a zest and originality that has never been surpassed, and from which he earned a considerable amount of money.

For the rest of his life he contributed puzzle columns to many periodicals. After his death, his son collected together the best of Sam Loyd's puzzles and published them in book form as the *Cyclopedia of Puzzles* – possibly the largest and most interesting assemblage of puzzles ever to appear in one volume.

The following eight puzzles have been selected from that work and are typical of Loyd's mathematical puzzles.

## 108
## TWO-STROKE GOLF ★★

Everybody is playing golf now, and even the lazy ones who a few weeks ago declared how much pleasanter it was to swing in a shady hammock have caught the golf fever and are chasing the ball around the golf links. I am not much of a golfer, but I have met a genius who has a winning system based on mathematics. He says: 'Just cultivate two strokes of different lengths, one a drive, the other an approach, and play directly towards the hole so that a combination of the two distances will get you there.'

What should be the proper lengths of strokes to learn that would make possible the lowest score on a nine-hole course, of 150 yards (137 metres), 300 yards (274 metres), 250 yards (229 metres), 325 yards (297 metres), 275 yards (251 metres), 350 yards (320 metres), 225 yards (206 metres), 400 yards (366 metres), and 425 yards (389 metres)? The ball must go the full length on each stroke, but you may go beyond the hole with either stroke, then play back towards the hole. All strokes are on a straight line towards the hole.

## 109
## THE CAT AND DOG RACE ★★

Many years ago, when Barnum's Circus was of a truth 'the greatest show on earth', the famous showman got me to prepare for him a series of prize puzzles for advertising purposes. They became widely known as the Questions of the Sphinx, on account of the large prizes offered to anyone who could master them.

Barnum was particularly pleased with the problem of the cat and dog race, letting it be known far and wide that on a certain first day of April he would give the answer and award the prizes, or, as he aptly put it, 'let the cat out of the bag, for the benefit of those most concerned'.

The wording of the puzzle was as follows:

'A trained cat and dog run a race, one hundred feet (30.5 metres) straightaway and return. The dog leaps three feet (one metre) at each bound and the cat but two feet (two thirds metre), but then she makes three leaps to his two. Now, under those circumstances, what are the possible outcomes of the race?'

The fact that the answer was to be made public on the first of April, and the sly reference to 'letting the cat out of the bag' was enough to intimate that the great showman had some funny answer up his sleeve.

## 110
## THE MISER'S PUZZLE ★★★

A certain miser, before he starved to death, hoarded up a quantity of five-, ten-, and twenty-dollar gold pieces. He kept them in five bags that were exactly alike in that each bag contained the same number of five-dollar pieces, the same number of ten-dollar pieces, and the same number of twenty-dollar pieces.

The miser counted his treasure by putting it all on the table, then dividing it into four piles that were also exactly alike in containing the same amounts of each type of coin. His final step was to take any two of these piles, put them together, then divide their coins into three piles which were exactly alike in the sense already explained. It should now be an easy matter to guess the least amount of money that this poor old man could have had.

## 111
## CARNIVAL DICE GAME ★★★

The following dice game is very popular at fairs and carnivals, but since two persons seldom agree on the chances of a player winning, I offer it as an elementary problem in the theory of probability.

On the counter are six squares marked 1, 2, 3, 4, 5, 6. Players are invited to place as much money as they wish on any one square. Three dice are then thrown. If your number appears on one die only, you get your money back plus the same amount. If two dice show your number, you get your money back plus twice the amount you placed on the square. If your number appears on all three dice, you get your money back plus three times the amount. Of course if the number is not on any of the dice, the operator gets your money.

To make this clearer with an example, suppose that you bet one dollar on No. 6. If one die shows a 6, you get your dollar back plus another dollar. If two dice show 6, you get back your dollar plus two dollars. If three dice show 6, you get your dollar back plus three dollars.

A player might reason: the chance of my number showing on one die is 1:6, but since there are three dice, the chances must be 3:6 or 1:2, therefore the game is a fair one. Of course this is the way the operator of the game wants everyone to reason, for it is quite fallacious.

Is the game favourable to the operator or the player, and, in either case, just how favourable is it?

## 112
## THE ANNUAL PICNIC ★★★

When they started off on the great annual picnic, every wagon carried exactly the same number of persons. Half way to the grounds ten wagons broke down, so it was necessary for each remaining wagon to carry one more person.

When they started for home it was discovered that fifteen more wagons were out of commission, so on the return trip there were three persons more in each wagon than when they started out in the morning.

How many people attended the great annual picnic?

## 113
## OLD BEACON TOWER ★★★★

Tourists who have taken a summer outing along the Jersey coast are familiar with the old Beacon Tower at Point Lookout. The ruins of the tower, which once served as a lighthouse for more than half a century, stand in the last stages of dissolution upon a little ledge of rocks that runs out into the sea. The county records show that it was originally 300 feet (91.5 metres) high, which was then a very respectable height indeed.

The centre support of the Beacon Tower was composed of huge poles skilfully spiked together, about which there wound a spiral staircase with an iron hand rail. This rail went exactly four times around the column. There was one baluster or picket to each step, and as these pickets were just one foot (0.3 metre) apart, it should really be a simple matter to determine how many steps one had to take to reach the top.

To summarize the data: the tower was 300 feet (91.5 metres) high from the ground to the top of the last step, the hand rail circled the tower four times, and the pickets in the rail, one to each step, were 1 foot (0.3 metre) apart. To this we must add that the diameter of the entire tower (that is, the diameter of the imaginary cylinder around which the rail twines) was twenty-three feet, ten and a half inches (72.7 metres). How many steps were on the circular staircase?

## 114
## THE ECCENTRIC TEACHER ★★★★

Here is a remarkable age problem which I am sure will amuse the young folks and at the same time open up a new line of reasoning for some of the wiseacres who make a speciality of statistical calculations.

It appears that an ingenious or eccentric teacher, as the case may be, desirous of bringing together a number of older pupils into a class he was forming, offered to give a prize each day to the side of boys or girls whose combined ages would prove to be the greatest.

Well, on the first day there was only one boy and one girl in attendance, and, as the boy's age was just twice that of the girl, the first day's prize went to the boy.

The next day the girl brought her sister to school. It was found that their combined ages were just twice that of the boy, so the two girls divided the prize.

When school opened the next day, however, the boy had recruited one of his brothers. It was found that the combined ages of the two boys were exactly twice as much as the ages of the two girls, so the boys carried off the honours that day and divided the prize between them.

The battle waxed warm now between the Jones and Brown families, and on the fourth day the two girls appeared accompanied by their elder sister; so it was then the combined ages of the three girls against the two boys. The girls won of course, once more bringing their ages up to just twice that of the boys. The struggle went on until the class was filled up, but our problem does not need to go further than this point. Tell me the age of that first boy, provided that the last young lady joined the class on her twenty-first birthday when she was exactly 7670 days old.

It is a simple but pretty puzzle, calling for ingenuity rather than mathematics and yielding readily to puzzle methods.

## 115
## FALSE WEIGHTS ★★★★★

The money of the East, coined in variable sizes and weights to facilitate the swindling of travellers, is too complex for our mathematicians to handle, so in describing the following manner of trading among the Orientals we will simplify matters by talking in dollars and cents.

Camels' hair, which enters largely into the manufacture of shawls and expensive rugs, is gathered by what is known as the common people and sold through a commission broker, in small or large lots, to the merchants. To ensure impartiality, the broker never buys for himself but, upon receiving an order to buy, finds someone who wishes to sell, and charges 2 per cent commission to each of them, thereby making 4 per cent on the transaction. Nevertheless, by juggling with the scales, he always manages to add to this profit by cheating, the more especially if a customer is green enough to place any confidence in his word or pious exclamations.

I take occasion to call attention to a pretty puzzle connected with a transaction which aptly illustrates the simplicity of his methods. Upon receiving a consignment of camels' hair he placed the same upon the short arm of his scales, so as to make the goods weigh one ounce (25 grammes) light to the pound (450 grammes), but when he came to sell it he reversed the scales so as to give one ounce to the pound (25 to 450 grammes) short, and thus made $25 by cheating.

It appears to be – and as a matter of fact is – a very simple problem, with clear and sufficient data for the purpose. Nevertheless, it will tax the cleverness of an expert book-keeper to figure out a correct answer to the question of how much the broker paid for the goods.

# H. E. DUDENEY

Henry Ernest Dudeney, who was born in Sussex in 1857, was undoubtedly the world's greatest composer of puzzles.

A first-rate amateur mathematician as well as an unparalleled puzzle creator, he contributed to a number of periodicals. For a while in the 1890s he collaborated with America's Sam Loyd, and on many occasions Loyd appealed to Dudeney for help with some of his more mathematically advanced puzzles.

For twenty years Dudeney had a puzzle page in *The Strand Magazine*, the same monthly magazine in which Sir Arthur Conan Doyle's Sherlock Holmes stories appeared. Four books containing collections of Dudeney's puzzles were published during his lifetime: *The Canterbury Puzzles* (1907), *Amusements in Mathematics* (1917), *The World's Best Word Puzzles* (1925) and *Modern Puzzles* (1926). After his death in 1930 two further collections were issued: *Puzzles and Curious Problems* and *A Puzzle-Mine*.

Here are nine of my favourite Dudeney number puzzles.

## 116
## WEIGHING THE TEA ★★

A grocer proposed to put 20 lb of China tea into 2 lb packets, but his weights had been misplaced by somebody, and he could only find the 5 lb and 9 lb weights. What is the quickest way for him to do the business? We will say at once that only nine weighings are really necessary.

## 117
## A COMMON DIVISOR ★★

Here is a puzzle that has been the subject of frequent inquiries by correspondents, only, of course, the actual figures are varied considerably. A country newspaper stated that many schoolmasters have suffered in health in their attempts to master it! Perhaps this is merely a little journalistic exaggeration, for it is really a simple question if only you have the cunning to hit on the method of attacking it.

This is the question: Find a common divisor for the three numbers 480,608, 508,811 and 723,217 so that the remainder shall be the same in every case.

## 118
## COW, GOAT AND GOOSE                                              ★★

A farmer found that his cow and goat would eat all the grass in a certain field in forty-five days, that the cow and the goose would eat it in sixty days, but that it would take the goat and the goose ninety days to eat it down. Now, if he had turned cow, goat and goose into the field together, how long would it have taken them to eat all the grass?

   Sir Isaac Newton showed us how to solve a puzzle of this kind with the grass growing all the time; but, for the sake of greater simplicity, we will assume that the season and conditions were such that the grass was not growing.

## 119
## A FAIR DISTRIBUTION                                              ★★★

A shopkeeper had oranges of three sizes for sale – one a penny, two a penny, and three a penny. So, of course, two of the second size, or three of the third size, were considered equal to one orange of the first size. Now a lady, who had an equal number of boys and girls, gave her children seven pence to be spent among them all on these oranges. The puzzle is to give each child an equal distribution of oranges. How was the seven pence spent, and how many children were there? No oranges may be cut. Do not jump hastily at the conclusion that there are several equally correct answers, for there is really only one solution.

## 120
## THE SEE-SAW PUZZLE                                               ★★★

Necessity is, indeed, the mother of invention. I was amused the other day in watching a boy who wanted to play see-saw and, in his failure to find another child to share the sport with him, had been driven back upon the ingenious resort of tying a number of bricks to one end of the plank to balance his weight at the other.

   As a matter of fact, he just balanced against sixteen bricks, when these were fixed to the short end of plank, but if he fixed them to the long end of plank he only needed eleven as balance.

   Now, what was that boy's weight, if a brick weighs equal to a three-quarter brick and three-quarters of a pound (0.34 kilogram)?

## 121
## THE DISPATCH RIDER                                               ★★★

If an army forty miles long advances forty miles while a dispatch rider gallops from the rear to the front, delivers a dispatch to the commanding general, and returns to the rear, how far has he to travel?

## 122
## THE TOWER OF PISA                                    ★★★

'When I was on a little tour in Italy, collecting material for my book on *Improvements in the Cultivation of Macaroni*,' said the Professor, 'I happened to be one day on the top of the Leaning Tower of Pisa, in company with an American stranger. "Some lean!" said my companion. "I guess we can build a bit straighter in the States. If one of our skyscrapers bent in this way there would be a hunt round for the architect."

'I remarked that the point at which we leant over was exactly 179 feet (54.5 metres) from the ground, and he put to me this question: "If a rubber ball was dropped from here, and on each rebound rose exactly one-tenth of the height from which it fell, can you say what distance the ball would travel before it came to rest?" I found it a very interesting proposition.'

## 123
## HOW OLD WAS MARY?                                    ★★★★

The combined ages of Mary and Ann are forty-four years and Mary is twice as old as Ann was when Mary was half as old as Ann will be when Ann is three times as old as Mary was when Mary was three times as old as Ann. How old is Mary?

That is all, but can you work it out? If not, ask your friends to help you, and watch the shadows of bewilderment creep over their faces as they attempt to grasp the intricacies of the question.

## 124
## MONKEY AND PULLEY                                    ★★★★

Here is a funny tangle. It is a mixture of Lewis Carroll's 'Monkey Puzzle', my own 'How old was Mary?' and some other trifles. But it is quite easy if you have a pretty clear head.

A rope is passed over a pulley. It has a weight at one end and a monkey at the other. There is the same length of rope on either side and equilibrium is maintained. The rope weighs four ounces per foot (113 grammes per 0.3 metre). The age of the monkey and the age of the monkey's mother together total four years. The weight of the monkey is as many pounds (kilogrammes) as the monkey's mother is years old. The monkey's mother is twice as old as the monkey was when the monkey's mother was half as old as the monkey will be when the monkey is three times as old as the monkey's mother was when the monkey's mother was three times as old as the monkey. The weight of the rope and the weight at the end was half as much again as the difference in weight between the weight of the weight and the weight of the weight and the weight of the monkey.

Now, what was the length of the rope?

# 3.

# RIDDLES, ENIGMAS AND CONUNDRUMS

## RIDDLES

Riddles have perhaps the longest pedigree of any type of puzzle. They were popular in most ancient civilizations – among the Babylonians, the Hebrews, the Egyptians, the Greeks, the Romans, the Persians and the Arabs.

Basically, a riddle consists of a fanciful or metaphorical description of something and the listener or reader is challenged to discover what it is that is being so described.

The well-known nursery rhyme *Humpty Dumpty* was originally a riddle.

Humpty Dumpty sat on a wall,
Humpty Dumpty had a great fall.
All the King's horses and all the King's men
Couldn't put Humpty together again.

The answer of course is *an egg* (though it might be objected that any object which might be irreparably damaged by a fall – a crystal vase, say – would equally fit the riddle).

## 125
## THE TRAVELLERS ★★

We travel much, yet prisoners are,
And close confined to boot;
We with the swiftest horse keep pace,
Yet always go on foot.

## 126
## OLD MOTHER TWITCHETT ★★

Old Mother Twitchett, she had but one eye,
And a great long tail that she let fly;
And every time she went through a gap,
She left a bit of her tail in the trap.

## ·127
## THE BEGINNING OF ETERNITY ★★

The beginning of eternity,
The end of time and space,
The beginning of every end,
The end of every race.

## 128
## THE RIDDLE OF THE SPHINX

'What creature is it that walks in the morning on four feet, at noon upon two, and in the evening on three?'

The Sphinx (of Thebes) put this riddle to all who happened to pass, and devoured anyone unable to answer it correctly. Nobody succeeded until Oedipus came along and gave the correct solution: 'Man, who creeps on the ground with hands and feet when an infant, walks erect in the middle of his life, and in old age walks with a stick.' The Sphinx, her secret revealed, threw herself headlong into the sea, and Oedipus was rewarded by being made King of Thebes.

(As a reward for his puzzle-solving ability he also had a complex named after him.)

## 129
## THE RIVAL BROTHERS ★★★

No twins could e'er with us compare,
    So like in shape and size;
Our bodies are like ermine fair,
    As black as jet our eyes:
But tho' so like in ev'ry feature,
    We rival brothers be;
Yet so obdurate is our nature,
    We often disagree.

# THE BOOKE OF MERRY RIDDLES

*The Booke of Merry Riddles* appeared in several editions in England during the sixteenth century. It was very popular, and is referred to in Shakespeare's play *The Merry Wives of Windsor*. Here are the first two riddles from this book.

## 130
### TWO LEGS SAT UPON THREE LEGS ★★

Two legs sat upon three legs, and had one leg in her hand; then in came four legs, and bare away one leg; then up start two legs, and threw three legs at four legs, and brought again one leg.

## 131
### HE WENT TO THE WOOD ★★

He went to the wood and caught it,
He sat him down and sought it;
Because he could not find it,
Home with him he brought it.

---

### Quizzical Quote

'The only literary pursuit which engaged Harriet at present, the only mental provision she was making for the evening of life, was the collecting and transcribing all the riddles of every sort that she could meet with into a thin quarto of hot-pressed paper, made up by her friend, and ornamented with cyphers and trophies. . . . Mr Elton was the only one whose assistance she asked. He was invited to contribute any really good enigmas, charades, or conundrums, that he might recollect; and she had the pleasure of seeing him most intently at work with his recollections; and at the same time, as she could perceive, most earnestly careful that nothing ungallant, nothing that did not breathe a compliment to the sex, should pass his lips. They owed to him their two or three politest puzzles.'

*Jane Austen*

# ENIGMAS

In one sense, the word *enigma* can be used to describe any puzzle. However, in a specialized sense the word is used to describe a riddle, usually in verse, which has pretensions to literary style.

Enigmas had a great vogue in the eighteenth and nineteenth centuries, and many notable figures tried their hand at them.

## 132
## AN ENIGMA BY JONATHAN SWIFT ★★

Jonathan Swift, the author of *Gulliver's Travels*, composed many enigmas, such as this one.

> From India's burning clime I'm brought,
> With cooling gales like zephyrs fraught.
> Not Iris, when she paints the sky,
> Can show more different hues than I;
> Nor can she change her form so fast,
> I'm now a sail, and now a mast.
> I here am red, and there am green,
> A beggar there and here a queen.
> I sometimes live in house of hair,
> And oft in hand of lady fair.
> I please the young, I grace the old,
> And am at once both hot and cold.
> Say what I am then, if you can,
> And find the rhyme, and you're the man.

## 133
## AN ENIGMA BY HORACE WALPOLE ★★★

Horace Walpole, the eighteenth-century English politician and man of letters, was very fond of enigmas, charades and other puzzles.

> Before my birth I had a name,
> But soon as born I chang'd the same;
> And when I'm laid within the tomb,
> I shall my father's name assume.
> I change my name three days together
> Yet live but one in any weather.

## 134
## AN ENIGMA BY VOLTAIRE ★★

What, of all things in the world, is the longest and the shortest, the swiftest and the slowest, the most divisible and the most extended, the most neglected and the most regretted; without which nothing can be done; which devours all that is little and ennobles all that is great?

## 135
## 'TWAS WHISPERED IN HEAVEN ★★

This enigma has often been attributed to the English poet Lord Byron, but it was in fact composed by Catherine Fanshawe in about 1814.

'Twas whisper'd in heaven, 'twas muttered in hell,
And echo caught faintly the sound as it fell;
On the confines of earth 'twas permitted to rest,
And the depths of the ocean its presence confess'd;
'Twill be found in the sphere, when 'tis riven asunder;
'Tis seen in the lightning, and heard in the thunder;
'Twas allotted to man from his earliest breath,
It assists at his birth, and attends him in death;
Presides o'er his happiness, honour and health,
Is the prop of his house, and the end of his wealth;
In the heaps of the miser 'tis hoarded with care,
But is sure to be lost in his prodigal heir;
It begins every hope, every wish it must bound;
It prays with the hermit, with monarchs is crown'd;
Without it the soldier and seaman may roam,
But woe to the wretch that expels it from home!
In the whispers of conscience 'tis sure to be found,
Nor e'en in the whirlwind of passion is drown'd;
'Twill soften the heart, but, though deaf to the ear,
'Twill make it acutely and constantly hear;
But, in short, let it rest; like a beautiful flower,
Oh! breathe on it softly, it dies in an hour.

---

**Quizzical Quote**

'It is a riddle wrapped in a mystery inside an enigma; but perhaps there is a key.'

*Winston Churchill*

---

# CONUNDRUMS

The form of riddle which is most popular today is the conundrum, defined by Dr Samuel Johnson as 'a quibble, a low jest, a play upon words'.

A conundrum is judged to be fine if it can be answered with a sentence which is punnish!

## 136
## CAN YOU TELL ME WHY? ★★

Can you tell me why
A hypocrite's eye
Can better descry
Than you or I
On how many toes
A pussycat goes?

## 137
## ALPHABETICAL CONUNDRUMS ★★★

These conundrums were originally posed by H. E. Dudeney. See how many you can solve.

Why is A like noon?

Why is B like a fire?

Why is C like a schoolmistress?

Why is D like a promontory?

Why is E like death?

Why is F like Paris?

Why is G like plum cake?

Why is H good for deafness?

Why is I the happiest?

Why is J like your nose?

Why is K like a pig's tail?

Why is L like giving a sweetheart away?

Why is M a favourite with miners?

Why is N like a pig?

Why is O the only one of the five vowels that you can hear?

Why is P like a man's firstborn?

Why is Q like a guide?

Why is R like Richmond?

Why is S like a furnace in a battery?

Why is T like an island?

Why is U a miserable letter?

Why is V the spoony letter?

Why is W like scandal?

Why does X mean 'to join'?

Why is Y like a pupil?

Why is Z like a cage of monkeys?

## 138
## HISTORY MYSTERIES ★★★

1 Who was the fastest runner in history?

2 What did the ancient Egyptians do when it was dark?

3 Who was the best actor in the Bible?

4 Why didn't they have pocket calculators in Biblical times?

5 Why did Caesar cross the Rubicon?

6 What musical instrument did the ancient Britons play?

7 Why were the Dark Ages dark?

8 Who was the father of the Black Prince?

9 Why did Henry VIII have so many wives?

10 Where did King John sign Magna Carta?

11 When did the alphabet have only twenty-four letters?

12 Who fought in the desert, carrying a lamp?

## 139
## CAREER CONUNDRUMS ★★★

1 What happens when a dentist and a manicurist disagree?

2 How does a sailor get his clothes clean?

3 Why is an auctioneer always busy?

4 Why are bakers greedy?

5 When are dustman sad?

6 Why was the archaeologist a failure?

7 Why are waiters good at sums?

8 Why is a coal miner like a beautician?

9 What kind of clothes do solicitors wear?

10 Why are fishmongers mean?

11 Whose job is it to inspect rabbit holes?

12 When are clergymen useful?

## 140
## ANIMAL CRACKERS ★★★

1  What has black and white stripes and red spots?

2  What do polar bears eat?

3  What animal charges through the forest and puts other animals to sleep?

4  What do frogs drink?

5  Which creatures eat the least?

6  Why do bears have fur coats?

7  Why do cows have bells round their necks?

8  Why did the farmer call his cockerel Robinson?

9  Why do birds fly south in autumn?

10  Why is burying an elephant so difficult?

11  Why does a giraffe have a long neck?

12  How do you get in touch with a fish?

## 141
## WHAT'S THE DIFFERENCE? ★★★

1  What's the difference between a lion with toothache and a rainstorm?

2  What's the difference between a tailor and a groom?

3  What's the difference between a poor man and a feather bed?

4  What's the difference between a bad husband and a bad shot?

5  What's the difference between a woman and a postage stamp?

6  What's the difference between a pickpocket and a church bell?

7  What's the difference between an elephant and a flea?

8  What's the difference between a boxer and a man with a cold?

9  What's the difference between an angler and a lazy schoolboy?

10  What's the difference between an ornithologist and someone who can't spell?

11  What's the difference between an oak tree and a tight shoe?

12  What's the difference between a sunbather and a builder?

# 4.

# PUZZLES WITH EVERYDAY OBJECTS

## 142
## SUGAR LUMPS ★★

Can you place ten lumps of sugar in three tea-cups so that there shall be an odd number of lumps in every cup? Don't give it up as impossible, because it can certainly be done.

## 143
## SALT ★★

Sprinkle a little salt on a table top. Now, the puzzle is to remove the salt without touching it, blowing it or fanning it, and without touching the table.
  How do you do it?

## 144
## TYING THE KNOT ★★

You need a piece of string, two or three feet (approx. one metre) in length. The puzzle is this: how can you pick up one end of the string in each hand and tie a knot in the string without letting go of either end?

## 145
## CATCH 'EM ★★

Hold the stem of an empty wine-glass with your second, third and little fingers. With thumb and forefinger of the same hand hold two sugar lumps, one on top of the other.

  Now, get both sugar lumps into the glass, one after the other, without using your other hand. You may find it easy to toss the first lump and catch it in the glass but not so easy to catch the second lump without the first one flying out.

## 146
## A FUNNEL PUZZLE ★★

You are handed a plastic funnel and you are challenged to extinguish a lighted candle by blowing through the funnel.

It is an easy challenge if you set about it the right way. But what is the right way?

## 147
## LIFT THE ICE-CUBE ★★

Place an ice-cube in a glass of cold water. Now, take a piece of string and use it to lift the ice-cube out of the water. You must do it without touching the glass or the ice or the water with your hands.

## 148
## THE BOTTLED EGG ★★

You are shown an ordinary milk bottle containing an ordinary egg. The egg is much wider than the neck of the bottle, and the shell of the egg is intact.

How did the egg get into the bottle?

## 149
## FLOAT THE CORK ★★

You give a cork to a friend and ask him to place it in a glass of water so that it floats exactly in the centre. No matter how many times he tries, the cork will not stay in the centre but always moves to the side of the glass and stays there.

Then you show him how it is done. How *is* it done?

## 150
## SNAP! ★★

Can you snap a matchstick in half, using only your thumb and forefinger? You may think it sounds easy – and it is, but only if you know the secret.

## 151
## KEEP IT DRY ★★

Here is an effective party trick. You push a handkerchief into a tumbler and then claim that you can completely immerse the glass in a bowl of water without getting the handkerchief wet. Of course no one will believe you – until you show how it is done. How do you do it?

## 152
## AN OVERBLOWN PUZZLE ★★

A playing card is placed face down on the table, and you are challenged to turn the card over merely by blowing at it. How do you do it?

## 153
## A FINANCIAL BALANCE ★★

Fold a banknote in half lengthways and then stand it on the table so that it forms a tunnel in the shape of an inverted V. You now have to balance a coin on top of it. How do you do it?

## 154
## CUT! ★★

You tie one end of a piece of string to the handle of a cup. Tie the other end of the string to a door handle, and leave the cup dangling. Next, bet a friend that he cannot cut the string and still leave the cup suspended. You then show him how to do it.

How is it done?

## 155
## THE ODD KING ★★

In a typical pack of cards, three of the kings are portrayed with moustaches, and only one without. Can you say, without going to examine a pack of cards, which king is the odd one out: hearts, diamonds, spades or clubs?

## 156
## A TRICK WITH DICE ★★

Here is a neat little trick with dice, devised by H. E. Dudeney.

I ask you to throw three dice without my seeing them. Then I tell you to multiply the value on the first die by 2 and add 5; then multiply the result by 5 and add the value of the second die; then multiply the result by 10 and add the value of the third die. You give me the total, and I can at once tell you the values thrown with the three dice.

How do I do it?

## 157
## CUNNING COINS ★★

It is an amusing pastime to take a coin (you will need one that has a representation of a head on it) and try to find how many different objects are to be seen there.

Thus, if I asked you to find an animal, the correct answer would be the hare (hair). Now, can you find the following: (a) a place of worship, (b) part of a bottle, (c) part of a hill, (d) a personal pronoun, (e) part of a trunk, (f) part of a whip, (g) a couple of flowers?

## 158
## HEADS AND TAILS                                                      ★★

Place six coins in a row – the first three heads-up and the other three tails-up. Now, in three moves, moving two adjacent coins together at a time (but without turning them over), make a row of alternating heads and tails.

## 159
## BLOW!                                                                ★★

Lay a visiting card on top of a wide shallow wine-glass. Place a coin on top of the card. Now, can you blow the coin into the glass?

## 160
## COIN CROSS                                                           ★★

You lay down seven coins to form a cross. This counts five vertically and three horizontally.

```
        O
    O   O   O
        O
        O
        O
```

    You then challenge a friend in the following terms: change the positions of *two* coins – no more, no less – so as to make the horizontal and vertical arms contain the same number of coins.
    How is this to be done?

## 161
### THE PAPER BAND PUZZLE ★★

Take a strip of paper one inch (three centimetres) wide and one yard (one metre) long. You must join the ends to form a loop and then draw a pencil line along the middle of the strip all round the loop *on both sides of the paper.*

You are not allowed to lift the pencil from the paper or let the line stray from the centre and go over the edge.

How do you do it?

## 162
### FOUR IN A ROW ★★

Place twelve coins on the table so as to form six rows with four coins in each row.

## 163
### TURNOVER ★★

The drawer of a matchbox is placed upside down on the table, with the matchbox cover standing upright on top of it. You are challenged to turn the drawer and cover upside down so that the drawer is balanced on top of the cover. You must do this without touching the drawer.

Can you meet the challenge?

## 164
### THREE AND A HALF DOZEN ★★

Place six matchsticks on the table so as to make three and a half dozen.

## 165
### MATCHEMATICS ★★

Using eight matchsticks, can you prove that half of twelve is seven?

---

### Quizzical Quote

Thy genius calls thee not to purchase fame
In keen iambics, but mild anagram:
Leave writing plays, and choose for thy command
Some peaceful province in Acrostic Land.
Where thou mayest wings display and altars raise
And torture one poor word ten thousand ways.

*John Dryden*

## 166
## MORE MATCHEMATICS ★★

Using ten matchsticks, prove that 5 minus $^7/_{10}$ is equal to 4.

## 167
## A PUSH-OVER ★★

This is an excellent puzzle for trying out on guests at an informal party.

Kneel on the floor, with a matchbox in your left hand. Placing your right elbow on the floor immediately in front of your right knee, lay your forearm flat on the floor with fingers outstretched. Now stand the matchbox on its end just beyond your fingertips. Still kneeling, straighten up and place both arms behind your back.

What you have to do now is bend forward, arms behind your back, and push over the matchbox with your nose! Can you do it without sprawling face-down on the floor?

## 168
## HOW MANY LEFT ★★

The magician is blindfolded. A volunteer from the audience is asked to deal out two piles of cards – as many as he likes in each pile, provided that one pile contains fewer cards than the other – and to tell the magician the number by which the cards in the greater pile exceed the cards in the lesser pile.

The magician then gives the following instructions: remove four cards from the pile containing fewer cards (pile 1); now remove from the other pile (pile 2) as many cards as there are remaining in the first pile; finally, remove all the cards in pile 1.

The magician is then able to announce the number of cards remaining. How does he do it?

## 169
## A CIRCLE OF COINS ★★★

Place eight coins in a circle, all with the heads facing upwards. Start from any coin, and in a clockwise direction count one, two, three, four, and turn over the fourth coin so that it is tails-up. Start again from any coin remaining heads-up and repeat the process. Continue until all the coins have their tails facing upwards.

## 170
## A COIN TRICK ★★★

Take six coins in your left hand in a pile. Remove the top one and place it on the table, carry the second one to the bottom of the pile, place the third one on the table to the right of the other, carry the next one to the bottom of the pile, place the next one on the table, again to the right of the others, and so on. When you have finished, the line of coins on the table reading from the left should be alternately head, tail, head, tail, head, tail.

If you have found the trick of arranging the pile, and can get them in order without being noticed, it will perplex your friends when you show them 'how very simple it really is'.

## 171
## ORANGES AND APPLES ★★★

Place twelve plates in a circle. Leave two of the plates empty, and put oranges and apples alternately on the remaining plates.

Now take an orange and an apple from two adjacent plates, one in each hand, and transfer them to the two empty plates. Then take the contents of two more adjacent plates and transfer them to the two new empty plates in the same way. Continue thus until, in five transfers, you have all the oranges together and all the apples together, without a break, and two adjacent plates empty.

When making the transfers you are not allowed to cross your hands, so as to reverse the positions of the fruit, and both must be picked up, and deposited, at the same time.

## 172
## DOMINO 23 ★★★

From a set of dominoes take the 1:3 and the 2:3 and lay them on the table like this: 1:3, 3:2. With the dominoes in this order you can now add adjacent numbers to give you any number from 1 to 9.

| | |
|---|---|
| 1 = 1 | 6 = 3 + 3 |
| 2 = 2 | 7 = 1 + 3 + 3 |
| 3 = 3 | 8 = 3 + 3 + 2 |
| 4 = 1 + 3 | 9 = 1 + 3 + 3 + 2 |
| 5 = 3 + 2 | |

Note that you could not have used 1 + 2 to make 3 as the 1 and 2 are not adjacent.

Now, can you find four dominoes that you can lay out in such a way as to allow you to add adjacent numbers to give any number from 1 to 23? When laying out the dominoes you do not need to match the ends, placing 1 against 1, 2 against 2, and so on, as you would if you were playing an actual game of dominoes.

## 173
## THE TEN CARDS
★★★

Here is an amusing little puzzle game that is calculated to perplex the beginner. Place ten playing cards in a row, all face upwards. There are two players. The first player may turn down any single card he chooses, the second player can then turn down any single card or two adjacent cards, then the first player turns down any single or two adjacent cards, and so on. The player who turns down the last card wins. Remember that the first player, on his first move, must turn down a single, but afterwards either player can turn down either a single or two adjacent cards, as he pleases.

Does the first player or the second player have the best chance of winning? What is the best strategy?

## 174
## ROOK AND BISHOP
★★★

If a rook and a bishop are placed at random on two different squares of a chessboard, what is the probability that one piece threatens the other?

## 175
## CHESS ROUTES
★★★

Place any chess piece in the top left-hand square of a chessboard. It is allowed to move one square at a time – either down, to the right, or diagonally down and to the right.

If it travels all the way to the bottom right-hand square, how many different routes could it take to get there?

## 176
## THE TRAVELLING ROOK
★★★

A rook can move any number of squares horizontally or vertically. If you place a rook on one of the four centre squares of the chessboard, what is the minimum number of moves it needs to pass over all the squares on the board and return to its original square?

## 177
## THE PEBBLE GAME
★★★

This intriguing two-player game may be played anywhere at any time, using matches, coins, buttons or any other small objects instead of pebbles.

The two players place an odd number of pebbles, we will say fifteen, between them. Then each in turn takes one, two or three pebbles (as he chooses), and the winner is the one who gets the odd number. Thus, if you get seven and your opponent eight, you win. If you get six and he gets nine, he wins.

Ought the first or second player to win, and why? What difference does it make if the players start with thirteen pebbles instead of fifteen?

# SOLITAIRE

The puzzle-game of Solitaire has a long and interesting history. It is said to have been invented by a French count, while he was imprisoned in the Bastille. The German mathematician Gottfried von Leibnitz was an early Solitaire fan – he wrote about it in a letter in 1716, explaining that his method was to start at the end and to work out the moves in reverse sequence!

Solitaire is believed to have been introduced into Britain by French prisoners captured during the Napoleonic Wars, and many articles and books were written about it in the nineteenth century.

## 178
## SOLITAIRE ★★★

Solitaire is usually played on a board that has thirty-three holes for pegs or hollows for marbles. However, you can easily draw a board on paper, and for counters you can use buttons, pennies or pebbles.

This diagram may be used as a guide:

```
        1   2   3
        4   5   6
7   8   9  10  11  12  13
14  15  16  17  18  19  20
21  22  23  24  25  26  27
       28  29  30
       31  32  33
```

There are a number of Solitaire puzzles, but we will describe the most familiar one. You begin by placing a counter in every position except the centre, number 17. You can now proceed to clear the board by jumping one counter over another. Counters may move up, down or sideways (never diagonally) and must jump over one counter to an empty position beyond. Whenever a counter is jumped over in this way it is removed. The aim is to be left with just one counter in the centre position.

Have a go and see if you can do it.

# 5.

# WORD PUZZLES

## 179
## UPSIDE DOWN ★★

Can you think of a common four-letter English word which, when printed in capital letters, reads the same upside-down as it does the right way up? There is only one such word.

## 180
## CLICHÉS ★★

Here is an easy puzzle. Ten familiar clichés have been muddled up. All you have to do is sort them out. How quickly can you do it?

(a) Gild the bucket

(b) Bury the lion

(c) Run the tables

(d) Beat about the music

(e) Face the lily

(f) Spill the gauntlet

(g) Kick the line

(h) Beard the bush

(i) Turn the hatchet

(j) Toe the beans

---

**Quizzical Quote**

'What good are brains to a man? They only unsettle him.'

*P. G. Wodehouse*

---

## IN WHOLE AND IN PART ★★

1 Replace the asterisks by the name of a bird to give the name of a bird:
   BIT★★★★

2 Replace the asterisks by the name of a bird to give the name of a bird:
   ★★★★★★★HAWK

3 Replace the asterisks by the name of a flower to give the name of a flower:
   PRIM★★★★

4 Replace the asterisks by the name of a composer to give the name of a
   composer: OFFEN★★★★

5 Replace the asterisks by the name of a composer to give the name of a
   composer: MONTE★★★★★

## 182
## TOM CAN PAW TAR ★★

The four 3-letter words in the title of this puzzle have a feature in common that is not shared by many other words. What is it?

## 183
## TRIPLETS ★★

| AGE | AIL | ANT | ASS | ATE | BID | CAN |
|-----|-----|-----|-----|-----|-----|-----|
| CAR | DEN | DID | ERA | FAT | FOR | GEN |
| GOD | HER | PAR | PEN | SON | TOR | TRY |

Arrange these 21 three-letter words into groups of three to form 7 nine-letter words (for example, CAB-LEG-RAM).

## 184
## MISSING VOWELS ★★

Here is a list of words that have had their vowels removed. Can you add the vowels and complete the words so as to match the definitions given? Each word needs three vowels added to it.

(a) PR   A musical play

(b) NN   A vegetable

(c) H    An American state

(d) DH   Another American state

(e) S    An English river

(f) B    A musical instrument

(g) ZR   An African country

(h) NC   A unit of weight

(i) SS   A desert watering-place

(j) RNG  A fruit

# LINKWORDS

★★

The answer to each clue is a five-letter word, and each answer differs from the previous one by only one letter.

| | | | | | |
|---|---|---|---|---|---|
| (a) | Unadorned | (g) | Pile | (m) | Ruse |
| (b) | Killed | (h) | Adhere | (n) | Moment |
| (c) | Discolour | (i) | Glib | (o) | Vestige |
| (d) | Sedate | (j) | Fit into place | (p) | Deal |
| (e) | Be upright | (k) | Young bird | (q) | Class |
| (f) | Smelled badly | (l) | Dense | (r) | Clearing |

# HIDDEN COUNTRIES

★★

In the sentence, 'Rome is the most interesting capital you will visit on your tour,' the word ITALY is hidden – in the last four letters of 'capital' and the first letter of 'you'.

Can you find the hidden country in each of the following sentences?

(a) For breakfast I boiled an egg and put a kipper under the grill.

(b) These little boats can tug a battleship or tug a liner.

(c) Are New Delhi and Karachi less popular than Calcutta and Islamabad?

(d) In the rock-pool I found a starfish, a sea-urchin and a spiny lobster.

(e) The islands are very fertile, with tall grass and fine palm-trees.

(f) The meal consisted of crabmeat, rice, pineapple, chicken, yams, coconut and peppers.

(g) If you are motoring and you spot hitch-hikers, do you give them a lift?

(h) Mary bought an ormolu coffee-table, a fine rug and a brass candlestick.

(i) Before going to the dance you have to brush your hair and polish your shoes.

(j) My grandmother will be ninety-nine on her next birthday.

---

### Quizzical Quote

'I am a Bear of Very Little Brain, and long words Bother me.'
*A. A. Milne*

---

Some words go together like a horse and carriage. Can you supply the 'carriages' for the following 'horses'?

(a)  Aches and _____

(b)  Bag and _____

(c)  Beck and _____

(d)  Cut and _____

(e)  Decline and _____

(f)  Fast and _____

(g)  Fine and _____

(h)  High and _____

(i)  Law and _____

(j)  Might and _____

(k)  Nook and _____

(l)  Pomp and _____

(m)  Stuff and _____

(n)  Tar and _____

(o)  Time and _____

(p)  Vim and _____

Choose from this list: baggage, call, circumstance, cranny, dandy, fall, feather, loose, main, mighty, nonsense, order, pains, thrust, tide, vigour.

# REBUSES

A rebus is a sort of hieroglyphic puzzle in which words or phrases are represented in a punning manner using either pictures or letters.

Pictorial rebuses were at one time a very popular form of puzzle for children. For example, the word 'I' would be represented by the drawing of an eye; the word 'and' would be represented by a drawing of a hand together with a letter H with a line through it.

More interesting, in my view, is the type of rebus that uses only letters, numbers and typographical symbols. For example:

OF-OF-OF-OF-OF-OF-OF-OF-OF-OF

This, of course, represents the word 'oftentimes'. Or how about this old favourite?

IF **B** MT PUT :

IF **B** . PUTTING :

You should read this as, 'If the grate be empty, put coal on. If the grate be full, stop putting coal on.'

## 188
## REBUS MOTTOES ★★

        and

(a)   standing towering man judges man.

      The     mind


(b)   There is an vice difference virtue.

       whelming

## 189
## A REBUS ADDRESS ★★

Can you make sense of this address?

WOOD

JOHN

HANTS.

## 190
## A RIOT OF REBUSES ★★★

See if you can work out what word or phrase is represented by each of these rebuses.

(a)  DNUOR

(b)  BOLT
      TH

(c)  ME
     AL

(d)  B         E         D

(e)  JOANB

(f)  ONCE
     10AM

## 191
## SHAKESPEAREAN REBUSES ★★★

(a)  Here is the title of a play by Shakespeare. What's the play?

MUCNILHADO

(b)  Here is a quotation from *Hamlet*. What's the quotation?

KINI

# TOM HOOD

Thomas Hood (1799–1845) was a popular poet who wrote a good deal of humorous verse, including the immortal lines:

> 'They went and told the sexton,
> And the sexton tolled the bell.'

His son, Thomas Hood the younger (1835–1874), known as Tom Hood, was equally popular in Victorian England. He edited a comic paper called *Fun*, which included lots of word puzzles and picture puzzles. After his death, a charming collection of his puzzles was published as *Excursions into Puzzledom, by the late Tom Hood & His Sister*. This book is full of all the types of puzzles that the Victorian public loved: rebuses, enigmas, riddles, acrostics, charades, etc.

## 192
### GHOTI ★★★

How do you think the title of this puzzle should be pronounced?

## 193
### AS EASY AS ABC ★★★

The answer to each clue below is a word containing the letters A, B and C in alphabetic sequence (but not *just* in alphabetic sequence) – as in the word '*al*ph*ab*eti*c*'.

   (a)   A counting-frame

   (b)   Language spoken in the Middle East

   (c)   Conveyance for sick or injured people

   (d)   A type of soap

   (e)   An old-fashioned tourist coach

   (f)   To kidnap

   (g)   The little grebe

## OFF WITH THEIR HEADS ★★★

Find the correct word to fit the first clue in each pair and then simply remove the first letter to find a word that fits the second clue.

For example, the answers to the first pair of clues are LAWFUL and AWFUL.

(a) Legal; terrible
(b) Religious festival; flower
(c) Imprecise; fever
(d) Cad; aquatic mammal
(e) Brave; fortunate
(f) Sausage; wrath
(g) Insular character; defamation
(h) Speech; share
(i) Buccaneer; enraged
(j) Fireside; planet

(k) Cripple; goal
(l) Female relative; loosen
(m) Spring; weight
(n) Flirtation; partnership
(o) Erudite; merited
(p) Furnish; jest
(q) Ox-like; sheep-like
(r) Uselessness; usefulness
(s) Concealed; not concealed

## MORE THAN ONE ★★★

Can you write down the plural of each of the following words?

(a) Teaspoonful
(b) Potato
(c) Datum
(d) Crisis
(e) Manservant

(f) Phenomenon
(g) Ox
(h) Piccolo
(i) Court-martial
(j) Madam

## SOUNDS THE SAME ★★★

Each pair of clues defines a pair of homonyms – that is, words that have the same sound but are spelt differently – RAYS and RAISE, for example. Can you identify all the pairs of homonyms?

(a) Arguments; awaken
(b) Floor; tale
(c) Sweet; abandon
(d) Location; quote
(e) Location; fish
(f) Atmosphere; inheritor

(g) Trees; gorse
(h) Pull; room
(i) Cry; sphere
(j) Fly; painful
(k) Inlets; cloth
(l) Pipe; took evasive action

In 1879 Lewis Carroll wrote to the editor of the magazine *Vanity Fair*, describing a new type of word puzzle that he had just devised:

'The rules of the Puzzle are simple enough. Two words are proposed, of the same length; and the Puzzle consists in linking these together by interposing other words, each of which shall differ from the next word in one letter only. That is to say, one letter may be changed in one of the given words, then one letter in the word so obtained, and so on, till we arrive at the other given word. The letters must not be interchanged among themselves, but each must keep to its own place. As an example, the word "head" may be changed into "tail" by interposing the words "heal, teal, tell, tall". I call the two given words "a Doublet", the interposed words "Links", and the entire series "a Chain", of which I here append an example:

| H | E | A | D |
|---|---|---|---|
| h | e | a | l |
| t | e | a | l |
| t | e | l | l |
| t | a | l | l |
| T | A | I | L |

It is, perhaps, needless to state that it is *de rigueur* that the links should be English words, such as might be used in good society.'

As a result of this letter, many of Lewis Carroll's Doublets were published in *Vanity Fair*. Here is a selection of them. It should be noted that all the links have to be words that can be found in a standard current dictionary. Proper nouns, archaic and dialect words are not permitted.

    (a)   Change WET to DRY  (*3 links*)

    (b)   Cover EYE with LID  (*3 links*)

    (c)   Change OAT to RYE  (*3 links*)

    (d)   Make TEA HOT  (*3 links*)

    (e)   Drive PIG into STY  (*4 links*)

    (f)   Change FISH to BIRD  (*4 links*)

    (g)   REST on SOFA  (*4 links*)

    (h)   Change TEARS into SMILE  (*5 links*)

    (i)   Turn POOR into RICH  (*5 links*)

    (j)   Evolve MAN from APE  (*5 links*)

(k)  Make FLOUR into BREAD   (*5 links*)

(l)  Get COAL from MINE   (*5 links*)

(m)  Raise FOUR to FIVE   (*6 links*)

(n)  Make WHEAT into BREAD   (*6 links*)

(o)  Run COMB into HAIR   (*6 links*)

(p)  Change BLACK to WHITE   (*6 links*)

(q)  Make BREAD into TOAST   (*6 links*)

(r)  Get WOOD from TREE   (*7 links*)

(s)  Prove GRASS to be GREEN   (*7 links*)

(t)  Combine ARMY and NAVY   (*7 links*)

(u)  Raise ONE to TWO   (*7 links*)

(v)  Change BLUE to PINK   (*8 links*)

(w)  Change GRUB to MOTH   (*9 links*)

(x)  Trace RIVER to SHORE   (*10 links*)

(y)  Turn WITCH into FAIRY   (*12 links*)

## 198
## ANAGRAM VERSE – 1     ★★★

Fill in the blanks in this little poem with five different four-letter words, all formed with the same letters.

> A ———— old woman, with ———— intent,
> Put on her ———— and away she went.
> 'Oh, ————,' she cried, 'give me today
> Something on which to ————, I pray.'

## 199
## ANAGRAM VERSE – 2     ★★★

Fill in the blanks in this little poem with four different four-letter words, all formed with the same letters.

> No ———— was there with cheerful light;
> The ———— raced round the ship all night.
> With ———— and wiles the sailors sought,
> But by the ———— not one was caught.

## ANAGRAM VERSE – 3 ★★★

Fill in the blanks in this little poem with five different four-letter words, all formed with the same letters.

> Landlord, fill the flowing – – – –
> Until the – – – – run over.
> Tonight we – – – – upon the – – – –,
> Tomorrow go to Dover.

## ABC ANAGRAMS ★★★★

Rearrange the letters in each of these words to form a word beginning with the letter A.

| | | | |
|---|---|---|---|
| (a) | IDOLATRY | (e) | LAMENTING |
| (b) | MARGINAL | (f) | CANONISES |
| (c) | SARDINES | (g) | STAGNATION |
| (d) | NEATHERD | (h) | EARTHBORN |

Rearrange the letters in each of these words to form a word beginning with the letter B.

| | | | |
|---|---|---|---|
| (i) | ABRIDGE | (m) | GABARDINE |
| (j) | SCHUBERT | (n) | REDBREAST |
| (k) | DOORBELL | (o) | GLIBNESS |
| (l) | CALIBRATE | (p) | SYBARITE |

Rearrange the letters in each of these words to form a word beginning with the letter C.

| | | | |
|---|---|---|---|
| (q) | SPECTRUM | (u) | SECTIONAL |
| (r) | SECONDING | (v) | OSCILLATION |
| (s) | MASCULINE | (w) | INCONSIDERATE |
| (t) | SCHEMATIC | (x) | SOLICITATION |

## 202
## THE END ★★★

The answers to the clues below are all words ending with the letters THE.

(a) To take a dip
(b) To dislike intensely
(c) To boil
(d) A river of the underworld
(e) Gay

(f) To squirm
(g) To dress
(h) To calm
(i) To respire
(j) A tool for mowing

## 203
## THE BEGINNING ★★★

The answers to all these clues are words beginning with the letters THE.

(a) A playhouse
(b) A sort of dictionary
(c) Instrument for measuring temperature
(d) City of ancient Greece or city of ancient Egypt
(e) A surveying instrument
(f) An ascending current of warm air
(g) The eighth letter of the Greek alphabet
(h) A month of the French Revolutionary calendar
(i) An actor
(j) Greek goddess of law and justice

---

### The First Prize Competition?

The first recorded prize competition is described in the Bible. Samson, at his wedding feast, offered to give thirty lengths of linen and thirty changes of clothing to the person who could correctly answer this riddle:

Out of the eater came something to eat;
Out of the strong came something sweet.

Samson was persuaded by his wife to tell her the answer. She treacherously told the Philistines, who were thus able to give the correct answer: a honeycomb in the body of a dead lion.

## 204
## SOUNDS BEASTLY ★★★

What you have to do here is find pairs of homonyms – that is, words that are pronounced the same but are spelt differently.

In each case, one word of the pair matches the definition given, and the other word is the name of a living creature – mammal, bird, fish, amphibian or insect. For example, the first pair are BARE and BEAR.

| | | | |
|---|---|---|---|
| (a) | Naked | (i) | To revolve |
| (b) | To exist | (j) | Connections |
| (c) | Costly | (k) | Unpolished |
| (d) | To run away | (l) | Innermost being |
| (e) | To drill a hole | (m) | Pulled along |
| (f) | Husky | (n) | To cry feebly |
| (g) | A filament growing from the skin | (o) | A half-moon |
| (h) | A Tibetan priest | | |

## 205
## AMERICAN ENGLISH ★★★

George Bernard Shaw called Britain and the USA two countries separated by the same language. There are, in fact, a great many differences between British English and American English. Here are fourteen British words and expressions that would cause bafflement if used in the USA. What are the American English equivalents?

| | | | |
|---|---|---|---|
| (a) | Braces | (h) | Postcode |
| (b) | Candy floss | (i) | Pushchair |
| (c) | Catapult | (j) | Receptionist |
| (d) | Foyer | (k) | Shop assistant |
| (e) | Full stop | (l) | Sweet shop |
| (f) | Ice lolly | (m) | Wardrobe |
| (g) | Nappy | (n) | Windscreen |

## 206
## TWO IN ONE ★★★

Can you find a single word which is a synonym for both words in each of the following pairs? For example, the first answer is SMART – in one sense, it means 'clever' and in another sense it means 'pain'.

(a) Clever; pain
(b) Draw; bond
(c) Thin; tend
(d) Bound; season
(e) Permission; vacate
(f) Near; shut

(g) Vessel; guile
(h) Occupation; ancestry
(i) Meditate; offspring
(j) Probe; intact
(k) Conclude; aim
(l) Moderate; passion

## 207
## FIND THE BIRDS ★★★★

Replace the asterisks by letters to reveal the names of fourteen birds found in Britain.

(a) *TAR**** _Starling_
(b) **INCH** _Chaffinch_
(c) *****WHAM***
(d) **SHAW*
(e) *HEAT***
(f) ****GRIN*
(g) *OTTER**

(h) *URNS****
(i) ***ORB***
(j) *WALL** _Swallow_
(k) ***STAR*
(l) *EDWIN* _Redwing_
(m) **THAT**
(n) **SKIN

## 208
## A SHORT VOCABULARY TEST ★★★★

Here are ten 2-letter words, all nouns, and all defined in *Chambers Twentieth Century Dictionary*.
How many of them can you define?

(a) ai
(b) da
(c) ea
(d) gu
(e) jo

(f) ka
(g) li
(h) od
(i) yu
(j) zo

## 209
## FOUR OF A KIND                                            ★★★★

What is the shortest word you can think of that contains:

(a)  four E's?              (f)  four F's?

(b)  four O's?              (g)  four G's?

(c)  four S's?              (h)  four T's?

(d)  four N's?              (i)  four A's?

(e)  four D's?              (j)  four Z's?

## 210
## MEANINGFUL NAMES                                          ★★★★

It is interesting to study the derivation of personal names. For instance, HAROLD means 'army rule' and both TABITHA and DORCAS mean 'a gazelle'.

Here, in the first column, are ten personal names. In the second column are their meanings – not, of course, in the right order. Can you match up each name with its meaning?

(a)  Algernon              Little she-bear

(b)  Bertram               Sunday

(c)  Bronwen               Bee

(d)  Dominic               Lover of horses

(e)  Donald                Laugh

(f)  Isaac                 White breast

(g)  Melissa               Bright raven

(h)  Philip                World chief

(i)  Rebecca               Moustached

(j)  Ursula                Noose

## 211
## ANIMAL ADJECTIVES

**★★★★**

If I were to ask you what animals the adjective 'equine' refers to, you would, of course, say 'horses'. Similarly, you would be able to tell me that 'canine' refers to 'dogs'.

Now, see if you can tell me what creatures the following adjectives refer to.

| | | | | | |
|---|---|---|---|---|---|
| (a) | accipitrine | (e) | cervine | (i) | ovine |
| (b) | anguine | (f) | lacertine | (j) | pavonine |
| (c) | anserine | (g) | lupine | (k) | ursine |
| (d) | caprine | (h) | murine | (l) | vulpine |

## 212
## WORD MIX

**★★★★**

1 Can you think of a common eight-letter English word that contains five vowels, one after the other?

2 Can you think of a common English word with three consecutive double letters?

3 Can you give me a nine-letter English word that contains only one vowel and consists of only one syllable?

4 Can you find a fifteen-letter English word, containing all the vowels, in which no letter is used more than once?

5 Can you find two eight-letter words that contain the first six letters of the alphabet?

The English language has many collective nouns for birds and animals. For example: a flock of sheep, a school of whales. And did you know that a number of geese on the ground should be called a gaggle, but the same geese in flight should be referred to as a skein? Some collective nouns are quite poetic – for example, a pride of lions, an exaltation of larks.

Can you supply the correct collective noun for each of these creatures?

| | | | | | |
|---|---|---|---|---|---|
| (a) | starlings | (h) | nightingales | (o) | turkeys |
| (b) | cats | (i) | foxes | (p) | rhinoceroses |
| (c) | kittens | (j) | ravens | (q) | seals |
| (d) | badgers | (k) | plovers | (r) | storks |
| (e) | owls | (l) | partridges | (s) | hares |
| (f) | apes | (m) | leopards | (t) | crows |
| (g) | peacocks | (n) | toads | | |

Choose your answers from the following list: cete, clowder, congregation, covey, crash, husk, kindle, knot, leap, murder, murmuration, mustering, ostentation, parliament, pod, rafter, shrewdness, skulk, unkindness, watch.

---

### Queen Victoria was not Amused

*The Private Life of the Queen* was published anonymously by 'One of Her Majesty's Servants' in 1897. In it appears the following passage:

'Her Majesty takes delight in a clever riddle or rebus, but on one occasion she was very angry at having been hoaxed over a riddle which was sent to her with a letter to the effect that it had been made by the Bishop of Salisbury. For four days the Queen and Prince Albert sought for the reply, when Charles Murray (Controller of the Household) was directed to write to the bishop and ask for the solution. The answer received was that the bishop had not made the riddle nor could he solve it.'

# CHARADES

In a Charade clues are given for the separate syllables of a word – 'my first', 'my second' and so on – and then for the word itself – 'my whole'. From these clues the solver has to identify the word in question.

Charades first became popular in the second half of the eighteenth century. The 1797 edition of the *Encyclopaedia Britannica* had this to say: 'The exercise of charades, if not greatly constructive, is at least innocent and amusing. At all events, as it has made its way into every fashionable circle, it will scarcely be deemed unworthy of attention.' They were certainly enjoyed by many of the most famous writers of that period – Sheridan, Walpole, Jane Austen and Maria Edgeworth, among others, write approvingly about Charades. The Rev Sydney Smith, however, declared that Charades were 'unpardonable trumpery' and said that those who indulged in them 'should instantly be hurried off to execution'!

From its origins as a written or printed word game the Charade was to develop into a popular parlour game in the nineteenth and early twentieth centuries, and later into an enjoyable TV panel game.

## 214
## A SIMPLE CHARADE                                                    ★★

My *first* is a sailor,
My *second*'s to gain;
My *whole*, though oft shot at,
Has never been slain.

## 215
## THE ARAB SHEPHERD                                                  ★★★

An Arab shepherd found my *first*
    In desert wastes astray,
He gave it food, he slaked its thirst,
And, in his bosom closely nursed,
    He carried it away.

Sad was its *second* to behold!
    It needed food and rest;
With fear it trembled, and with cold;
But soon the shepherd sought the fold
    And bore it in his breast.

The sky had neither moon nor star,
    As home his steps he bent;
But soon his troubles vanished are,
For clearly he beholds afar
    My *whole* within his tent.

## 216
## BESIDE THE BROOK ★★★

Beside the brook one summer day
　　When Nature all was merry,
I saw a gypsy maiden stray,
　　As brown as any berry;
She with the limpid waters quenched her thirst,
And picked a simple salad of my *first*.

The woodbine and the eglantine,
　　The woodruff and the mallow,
Delight to twine and intertwine
　　Beside that streamlet shallow;
And kissed by sunlight and caressed by dews,
My *second* in the air around diffuse.

The sun went down, the twilight fell,
　　Out shone the stars unnumbered;
Each floweret closed its honeyed cell,
　　And Nature softly slumbered.
While pale and cold across the heavens stole,
In modest maiden majesty, my *whole*.

## 217
## VERY FEMININE ★★★

My *whole* is a woman. Woman is my *end*, was my *beginning*, and you will always
find her in my *midst*.

## 218
## A SYLVAN CHARADE ★★★

My *first* will range the meadow through
　　In savage pride and state;
But should he make my *next* at you,
　　Your danger would be great.
My *whole* in russet cap is found,
　　And robe of lovely green,
Tall, springing from the marshy ground,
　　Like some bright fairy queen.

# DUDENEY'S WORD PUZZLES

H. E. Dudeney, the world's greatest puzzle inventor, has already been encountered in the chapter on Number Puzzles (pages 39–41). Although his interests were mainly mathematical, and he was most influential in this area of puzzledom, he did on occasion turn his hand to the construction of word puzzles. He was sixty-eight when his book *The World's Best Word Puzzles* was published in 1925. Many of the puzzles therein had previously appeared in *The Strand Magazine*.

The following nine puzzles by Dudeney are among my favourites.

## 219
## A SPARKLING PUZZLE ★★

Take the word SPARKLING and cover up or take away one letter so as to leave a new word. Then take away another letter from the new word and leave another word. Continue this, letter by letter, without changing their order, so as to get a new word every time, until you finally leave a word of only one letter.

## 220
## A BURIED QUOTATION ★★

In case any readers should happen to be unacquainted with the form of puzzle known as 'buried words', I will give an example. In the following couplet there are two buried towns:

>      In love inconstant I no pleasure find;
>      No fickle girl is bonny to my mind.

Here, if you start at the 'c' in 'inconstant', you get the word 'Constantinople', and beginning with the 'l' in 'girl' you have the second word 'Lisbon'. Now in the following paragraph is concealed a familiar quotation from Shakespeare, each word being buried in its proper order. Can you discover the sentence?

'Strange weather! What could equal it? Yesterday sunshine and soft breezes; today a summer cyclone raging noisily; then other changes, as floods of the fiercest rain eddy beneath the blast.'

## 221
## MORE MISSING WORDS ★★

>      I saw her dance like –––––– upon the green;
>          Her gown was white, with –––––– of yellow dyed;
>      Her cheeks were like the –––––– apple seen,
>          And now before the –––––– she stands, a bride.

The four missing words all contain the same six letters.

## 222
### YET MORE MISSING WORDS ★★

It is a time of ––––––, a time of evil;
  The starving seamstress with her –––––– doth toil,
And no man –––––– now to feast or revel,
  Or dream of –––––– and of war's turmoil.

The missing words contain the same six letters, differently arranged.

## 223
### AN ANGLING PASTIME ★★

In the following paragraph are concealed eighteen fishes. How many can you land? This is how you catch them. The words 'Mack ere long' conceal the word 'Mackerel', and the fish 'cod' will be caught in the words 'tobacco, Dick'. Now see if you can land the remaining sixteen.

'I expect Dick and Mack ere long – they are coming to supper, Charles,' said Mr Wilkins, walking to and fro. 'A cheerful fellow is Dick – never melancholy or sombre among his friends, but as bright as his prattling child. He is in that tram-car, perhaps, though he does not often choose that manner of travelling.' Dick soon arrived, and another ring at the bell brought Mack, who had a certain solemn air. He is reading for the Bar, believing that he has forensic power, though he really does not possess a whit. In golf he distinguished himself, but, if we take his word, fishing is his great point. Dick is very popular at routs and balls, and has such ubiquitous habits. 'Have some tobacco, Dick,' said Mr Wilkins, 'or a piece of this cake, which has almonds in it.'

## 224
### HIDDEN FRUITS ★★

Each of the following twelve lines of verse contains a hidden fruit. How many can you find?

Ah! If I get my good ship home
  I'll find a tempting rural spot,
Where mayhap pleasant flowers will bloom,
  And there I'll shape a charming cot.

Where bees sip nectar in each flower,
  And Philomel on hawthorn rests,
I'll shape a rustic, sun-kissed bower –
  A bower meet for angel guests.

Then she who lives and loves with me,
  Cheering our days of calm repose,
Sole monarch of the flowers will be –
  For Myra is indeed a rose.

# THE EXCURSION ★★★

Palindromic words read backwards and forwards the same – like Nan, Anna, Exe, Oxo, Glenelg, etc. None of these examples may be used in the following paragraph, where every blank must be filled by a different palindromic word to make sense. The dots here do not indicate the number of letters. Probably there are only about four words that will give the reader any trouble.

It was a lovely day, between . . . and . . ., when . . ., his sister . . ., and their father decided to . . . down to the meadow to have a . . . at their pet . . . 'Look, . . .,' said the children, 'there is a blue . . . in the tree. . . .! If it . . . us it will fly away, for it will soon have its . . . on us.' They called at a cottage to fetch a young . . . that they had bought, and had a . . . at the baby while they put on it a new . . . and made it some. . . . The children so worshipped the little . . . that they nearly . . . it. The boy was eating an orange, and allowed a . . . to fly in the eye of a demure . . . who appeared at the door. Her face grew . . ., and she said, '. . .! But I am sure you . . . it by an accident.' 'I am very sorry, . . .,' he replied. 'Of course, it was not an intentional. . . .' The lady did not further . . . to the matter. They then walked along the . . . seashore, to . . . out their time, and saw a ship in the distance with the captain on the . . . and they shouted '. . .!' The children were a little tired so they had a bathe, and found it an excellent. . . . The boy boasted of his swimming, and his father advised him to keep . . . on the subject, or he should have to . . . him, as he is apt to . . . on his own trumpet. They met a gentleman who was an alderman, or holder of some such . . . post, with whom the father discussed the question of the equality of the . . . and many a doctrine and . . . was uttered that seemed strange to their juvenile ears.

# BUILDING A WORD SQUARE ★★★

```
P   O   I   S   E   D
O   T   P   I   T   A
I   P   U   T   O   R
S   I   T   T   E   R
E   T   O   E   L   E
D   A   R   R   E   M
```

This would be a word square, if only all the lines and columns spelt real words which, with the exception of POISED and SITTER, they do not. The puzzle is to rearrange these letters so that a perfect word square may be formed.

As a clue I will state that all the letters in the diagonal – P, T, U, T, L, M – are correctly placed as they stand at present. Most of the other letters are out of their proper places.

# COMPLETE THE WORD SQUARE ★★★

Can you complete the construction of this word square by filling in the missing words? Every word is an English one in common use.

```
N   E   S   T   L   E   S
E       R           T
S       A           E
T   R   A   I   T   O   R
L       T           N
E       O           E
S   T   E   R   N   E   R
```

# DOUBLE ACROSTICS

The word *acrostic* is derived from the Greek and means 'first letter verse'. As a type of word puzzle acrostics originated in the nineteenth century, although acrostic verse forms – in which the initial letters of the lines of verse spell out a name – had been used for centuries before that.

In a Double Acrostic puzzle clues, which are usually in verse, are given to a number of words. If you solve these clues correctly, the first and last letters of the answers yield a pair of words which are the theme of the acrostic, and for which clues are also provided.

The first published Double Acrostic appeared in 1856. It was composed by the Rev J. Bradley who composed puzzles under the pseudonym Cuthbert Bede, and he described his acrostic as a type of puzzle 'lately introduced'. It is known that in the same year Queen Victoria composed one for her children at Windsor Castle, and it is even thought possible that the queen herself may have been the inventor of the Double Acrostic!

## 228
## THE FIRST PUBLISHED DOUBLE ACROSTIC ★★★

This puzzle by Cuthbert Bede appeared in the *Illustrated London News* on 30 August 1856, and was the first Double Acrostic ever to appear in print.

**The Words**
A mighty centre of woe and wealth;
   A world in little, a kingdom small.
A tainted scenter, a foe to health;
   A quiet way for a wooden wall.
Find out these words as soon as you can, sir,
And then you'll have found the Acrostic's answer.

**The Letters**
Untax'd I brighten the poor man's home –
   My wings wave over the beauty's brow –
I steal by St Petersburgh's gilded dome –
   While Bomba's subjects below me bow.
A Cook has reason to dread my name,
Though I carry the tidings of pride and shame.

## 229
## QUEEN VICTORIA'S ACROSTIC ★★★

The initial letters form the name of a town in England and the final letters (read upwards) what that town is famous for.

A city in Italy.
A river in Germany.
A town in the United States.
A town in North America.
A town in Holland.
The Turkish name for Constantinople.
A town in Bothnia.
A city in Greece.
A circle on the globe.

(Since the modern solver is probably at a disadvantage compared to the solver in 1856 when it comes to identifying towns in Bothnia, I will tell you that the answer to this clue is TORNEA.)

## 230
## AN ENGLISHMAN ★★

Here is a fairly easy Double Acrostic by H. E. Dudeney.

    The British type, we fancy in our folly.
    He's fat, bucolic, rubicund and jolly.
1  May you be just as patient as was he,
    Though not so poor, we wish most earnestly.
2  All is not gold that glitters, you believe;
    Then do not let its gilt your eyes deceive.
3  Producer of great melodies and art,
    Confuse not with piano-organ's part.
4  'Cetaceous mammal found in northern seas.'
    So says the dictionary, if you please.

Here is a very difficult Double Acrostic included by Carroll in his collection of poems entitled *Phantasmagoria* in 1869. Note the remarkable third stanza.

There was an ancient City, stricken down
    With a strange frenzy, and for many a day
They paced from morn to eve the crowded town,
    And danced the night away.

I asked the cause: the aged man grew sad:
    They pointed to a building gray and tall,
And hoarsely answered, 'Step inside, my lad,
    And then you'll see it all.'

Yet what are all such gaieties to me
    Whose thoughts are full of indices and surds?
$$x^2 + 7x + 53$$
$$= \frac{11}{3}.$$

But something whispered, 'It will soon be done:
    Bands cannot always play, nor ladies smile:
Endure with patience the distasteful fun
    For just a little while!'

A change came o'er my Vision – it was night:
    We clove a pathway through a frantic throng:
The steeds, wild-plunging, filled us with affright:
    The chariots whirled along.

Within a marble hall a river ran –
    A living tide, half muslin and half cloth:
And here one mourned a broken wreath or fan
    Yet swallowed down her wrath:

And here one offered to a thirsty fair
    (His words half-drowned amid those thunders tuneful)
Some frozen viand (there were many there),
    A tooth-ache in each spoonful.

There comes a happy pause, for human strength
    Will not endure to dance without cessation;
And every one must reach the point at length
    Of absolute prostration.

At such a moment ladies learn to give,
    To partners who would urge them overmuch,
A flat and yet decided negative –
    Photographers love such.

There comes a welcome summons – hope revives,
　And fading eyes grow bright, and pulses quicken:
Incessant pop the corks, and busy knives
　Dispense the tongue and chicken.

Flushed with new life, the crowd flows back again:
　And all is tangled talk and mazy motion –
Much like a waving field of golden grain,
　Or a tempestuous ocean.

And thus they give the time, that Nature meant
　For peaceful sleep and meditative snores,
To ceaseless din and mindless merriment
　And waste of shoes and floors.

And One (we name him not) that flies the flowers,
　That dreads the dances, and that shuns the salads,
They doom to pass in solitude the hours,
　Writing acrostic-ballads.

How late it grows! The hour is surely past
　That should have warned us with its double knock?
The twilight wanes, and morning comes at last –
　'Oh, Uncle, what's o'clock?'

The Uncle gravely nods, and wisely winks.
　It *may* mean much, but how is one to know?
He opes his mouth – yet out of it, methinks,
　No words of wisdom flow.

## 232
## A CRYPTIC ACROSTIC ★★★

Here is an old puzzle form in modern guise. The answers to the cryptic clues are all five-letter words, and the first and last letters of the answers spell out the names of two famous painters.

(a)　He does not trust in decency, niceness, etc.

(b)　Carmen, for example, knotting a rope.

(c)　Some funny long johns or a stocking.

(d)　Pea is changing colour.

(e)　Boy taking it back, going in and out.

(f)　Mabel goes for a stroll.

(g)　Most suitable environment for a creature.

(h)　The slightest sort of tales.

(i)　Muse – if you have time to.

# 6.

# CROSSWORDS

## THE BIRTH OF THE CROSSWORD

Arthur Wynne, who in 1905 had emigrated to the United States from his native Liverpool, was the editor of a weekly puzzle page in a newspaper called *The New York World*.

In December 1913 he was preparing a special Christmas edition of the puzzle page, and decided that it would be a good idea to try something new. The idea that he eventually came up with was a novel variation of the traditional word-square to which he gave the name WORD-CROSS. This was, in fact, the first crossword puzzle.

The crossword proved so popular with the readers that it became a permanent feature. The first few crosswords were diamond-shaped, but it soon evolved into the square format with which we are now so familiar. For the next decade *The New York World* was the only newspaper anywhere to have a regular crossword.

Here is the world's first crossword, compiled by Arthur Wynne, as it appeared in the Christmas edition of *The New York World* in 1913.

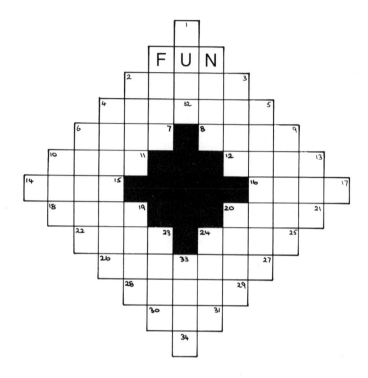

### Across

| | |
|---|---|
| 2–3 | What bargain hunters enjoy |
| 4–5 | A written acknowledgement |
| 6–7 | Such and nothing more |
| 10–11 | A bird |
| 14–15 | Opposed to less |
| 18–19 | What this puzzle is |
| 22–23 | An animal of prey |
| 26–27 | The close of a day |
| 28–29 | To elude |
| 30–31 | The plural of is |
| 8–9 | To cultivate |
| 12–13 | A bar of wood or iron |
| 16–17 | What artists learn to do |
| 20–21 | Fastened |
| 24–25 | Found on the seashore |

### Down

| | |
|---|---|
| 6–22 | What we all should be |
| 4–26 | A day dream |
| 2–11 | A talon |
| 19–28 | A pigeon |
| F–7 | Part of your head |
| 23–30 | A river in Russia |
| 1–32 | To govern |
| 33–34 | An aromatic plant |
| N–8 | A fist |
| 24–31 | To agree with |
| 3–12 | Part of a ship |
| 20–29 | One |
| 5–27 | Exchanging |
| 9–25 | Sunk in mud |
| 13–21 | A boy |
| 10–18 | The fibre of the gomuti palm |

# THE SECOND CROSSWORD

Following the success of his first crossword, Arthur Wynne produced this crossword the following week for the New Year edition of *The New York World*.

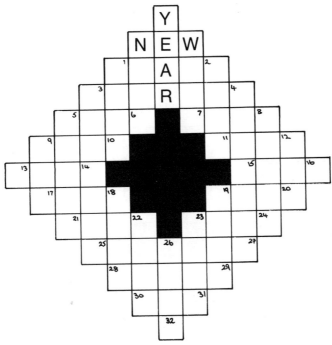

### Across
| | |
|---|---|
| **1–2** | Wild animals |
| **3–4** | Coating with tar |
| **5–6** | A grating |
| **7–8** | Conversation |
| **9–10** | An iron wedge |
| **11–12** | To bind |
| **13–14** | A young woman |
| **15–16** | Used as a gem |
| **17–18** | Ninety inches |
| **19–20** | To remain |
| **21–22** | A food chamber |
| **23–24** | To stagger |
| **25–27** | A number |
| **28–29** | Gull-like birds |
| **30–31** | The egg of an insect |

### Down
| | |
|---|---|
| **1–10** | Security for release |
| **3–25** | A lattice |
| **5–21** | Young women |
| **9–17** | Good to eat |
| **18–28** | To cut lengthwise |
| **N–6** | The German for North |
| **22–30** | Cattle |
| **26–32** | A journey |
| **W–7** | A summons |
| **23–31** | Torn |
| **2–11** | A hidden obstacle |
| **19–29** | Perceives |
| **4–27** | To sparkle |
| **8–24** | A Hottentot's home |
| **12–20** | Not wet |

Surely the strangest story in crossword history concerns the *Daily Telegraph*'s D-Day crosswords.

In the two weeks leading up to the Allies' invasion of Normandy on 6 June 1944, the *Daily Telegraph* crosswords contained almost a dozen of the top-secret codewords for the invasion – words such as Overlord, Pluto, Mulberry, Neptune. All these crosswords were compiled by one man, Leonard Dawe. Needless to say, Mr Dawe was subjected to an intensive grilling by counter-intelligence officers, but he was able to convince them that it was just an incredible coincidence and that he was not passing information to the enemy via his cryptic clues.

Here is one of the actual crosswords that were involved in that episode.

## Across

1 'Lid on slang' (anag.) (but is all 15 across so pure in speech?) (two words) (4, 6)
8 Doing nothing because there's nothing doing possibly (4)
10 The kind of constitution that laughs at doctors of the Goebbels type! (10)
11 Our supposed portion in 1940, but we never tumbled to it (4)
12 – though coming to the this of it (4)
15 Where the work of the architect stands very high (two words) (3, 4)
18 The girl who went into her own reflections very amusingly (5)
19 You must be plumb right! (5)
20 Just a note (5)
21 Got in wrongly to the bar (5)
22 Would this problem be a sitter to an artist? (5)
23 A joint affair (5)
24 Not a forbidding hue (5)
25 She is in an ancient city (official!) (5)
26 Of Eastern origin, but serious (7)
30 Cast a skin (4)
33 Points in favour of some players? (4)
34 A submarine should be, of course (10)
35 He gets his wings on false pretences (4)
36 Where to look for Maud's boyfriend? (two words) (6, 4)

## Down

2 Sign of appeal to men (4)
3 Cause of the hidden hand? (5)
4 Like a bear with a sore head (5)
5 He may be like the curate's egg, good in parts (5)
6 Outcast agents of fickle chance (4)
7 Flower one might well salute (4)
9 End of a term for losing cohesion (two words) (8, 2)
10 Those working in it are quite sunk in their work (6-4)
13 It may be seen at the front at feeding time (5-5)
14 See printer for an adventure (10)
15 Britannia and he hold to the same thing (7)
16 Sphere of 15 down (5)
17 An exclusive notice (two words) (4, 3)
20 The root of smokers' pleasures (5)
27 It comes from the rates – blooming scandal! (5)
28 Choice of directions of tongue (5)
29 Was an arm, or might support one (5)
31 No good man will live up to it (4)
32 Shoot to spot (4)
33 Finished! (4)

Here is a standard cryptic crossword by a great puzzle-setter, Michael Curl.

## Across

1 Monsters devouring insensitive fruit-growers (8)
5 Festival for oriental priests about the beginning of May (6)
9 What is inside is satisfying (8)
10 Dull food – for example, Dorothy's turnover (6)
11 A letter for the publican (8)
12 Odd traits of a painter, for example (6)
14 Be patient while I speak, my ursine companion (4,4,2)
18 Charitable people spoil one in the devil's clutches (10)
22 Claim member is taking drink out (6)
23 Cores may come from a tree (8)
24 Land-owners or young men circumventing the Inland Revenue (6)
25 Teach a learner to be casual (8)
26 National race around Northern Ireland (6)
27 Part of book extracted in theatre? (8)

## Down

1 Esoteric company turning to fringe religion (6)
2 Tins contain no clergymen (6)
3 Ancient Egyptians' leader cast in a precious metal (3-3)
4 Cleaners frighten off men (10)
6 Radio set fixed for a space traveller (8)
7 Ragtime for Cinders (8)
8 Enclosed warmth in a wooden building (8)
13 Biscuit or drink to go with game (6,4)
15 A fool suffered under attack (8)
16 Paint a bird followed by a cat around a pole (8)
17 GI's bread scattered for troops (8)
19 Learning about a Hindu's capital – it's in Pakistan (6)
20 Made for sea (6)
21 Unthinking reaction is more than obtuse (6)

And here is another puzzle by Michael Curl.

## Across

1 Inferior sort of gold ware (3-5)
5 Southern fish stink (6)
9 Double-Dutch offender? (8)
10 United Nations is getting on in harmony (6)
12 Churchman's general rule or principle (5)
13 Exclude soft drinks salesman (3-6)
14 Iris turned over no liquor-jug (6)
16 Confections of little importance? (7)
19 Survive longer but get dismissed finally (7)
21 A meeting place, in a way (6)
23 Chartism's movable feast (9)
25 Regulation – the alternative to red revolution? (5)
26 Use logic concerning a child (6)
27 This should take the boredom out of saving (8)
28 Eastern flower festival (6)
29 Lens care involved a detergent, perhaps (8)

## Down

1 Be in luck in a German port (6)
2 Slow giant breaking up railway sleepers (6-3)
3 Type of citizen (5)
4 Mr Hoffman holds second-rate trash can (7)
6 Oddly, green ain't orange (9)
7 Pried, so end is found out (5)
8 Barbarian with hair – a woman chaser? (8)
11 A little revolutionary has to move briskly (4)
15 A politician happy to receive fourteen pounds (9)
17 She washes Los Angeles strip (9)
18 Aircraft on line in the Church of England (8)
20 As far as I'm concerned, it's a book (4)
21 Where weapons are kept for the team (7)
22 A kitchen implement sounds more important (6)
24 Sheep take nothing in travels (5)
25 Fifty per cent of operations may be performed in theatre (5)

# ANAGRAM CROSSWORD

★★

In this crossword the clues are all anagrams. Simply rearrange the letters of each clue to make another word to be inserted in the diagram. Take care however. If the clue is PART, for example, then the solution could be either RAPT or TRAP – you must find some interlocking letters before you can decide which is the correct solution.

| Across | | | | Down | | | |
|---|---|---|---|---|---|---|---|
| 1 | Braids | 17 | Brigade | 1 | Issued | 13 | Saviour |
| 4 | Assist | 19 | Stone | 2 | Purse | 14 | Eroding |
| 8 | Panties | 21 | Organ | 3 | Engrave | 15 | Ranged |
| 10 | Weird | 22 | Trooped | 5 | Wrote | 16 | Hoarse |
| 11 | Grips | 23 | Duster | 6 | Manures | 18 | Needs |
| 12 | Taverns | 24 | Header | 7 | Teased | 20 | Sheet |
| 13 | Relatives | | | 9 | Statement | | |

## Crossword Crazy

In 1924 two young Americans named Simon and Schuster had set up a new publishing firm and were looking about for something to publish. They decided to publish a book of crossword puzzles that were at the time so popular a feature of *The New York World*. In doing so, they started a craze that was to sweep America.

Despite scepticism from booksellers and distributors, Simon and Schuster's first crossword book was published on 10 April 1924. With each book a free pencil was provided. Initial orders for the book amounted to no more than 800, but by the end of the year they had published two more crossword books and total sales were over 350,000.

America went crossword crazy. More and more newspapers printed crosswords. Crossword parties were held. Crossword competitions were held in such public arenas as the Hotel Roosevelt and Wanamaker's Auditorium in New York. Crosswords were put on the curriculum at the University of Kentucky. Because crosswords were so popular with rail travellers, the Baltimore and Ohio Railroad provided dictionaries on all its main-line trains. Ministers issued crosswords to their congregations in order to attract people to church. People consulting dictionaries in public reference libraries had to be rationed to five minutes each. Crossword jewellery was popular, and so were black and white checkered dresses. On Broadway a revue called *Puzzles of 1925* satirized the craze.

In Britain in December 1925 *The Times*, under the headline AN ENSLAVED AMERICA, reported on the crossword craze and calculated that 5 million hours daily of American people's time was 'wasted in this unprofitable trifling'.

The crossword had, however, already reached these shores. Britain's first crossword had been published in the *Sunday Express* on 2 November 1924 – compiled by none other than Arthur Wynne, creator of the original crossword – and the idea had spread to other newspapers.

Although the craze gradually abated, the crossword was definitely here to stay. The last bastion of resistance fell when, on 22 January 1930, *The Times* included its own first crossword.

This puzzle was created by 'Apex', alias Eric Chalkley, who has compiled lots of intriguing and entertaining crosswords.

Each Across clue is a passage from which the printer has removed a hidden answer, closing the gap, taking liberties sometimes with punctuation and spacing, but not disturbing the order of the remaining letters. *Example* 'Ximenes once had a solver in hobo, I'm told (4)': *Answer – Arts –* 'Ximenes once had a solver in Hobart, so I'm told'. Each passage when complete makes sense.

All the Down clues are normal cryptic ones.

## Across

1 An actor without, aping every Theatrical Agency (8)
7 A man who is angry and a lady for a fight (4)
8 After tests, wanted to play games with the hostess (4)
9 On hearing the burglar a lily-maid fled from the house (6)
11 After leaving the bread, going home to the wife (4)
14 BBC man in 'Peter' viewing South Americans for TV programme (4)
16 One listing the works of Sir Arthur, bit Ted a piece (6)
17 Some carpenters mind sot – hers simply butt them (4)
18 A shocking caller, remember of his own team, out in every match (4)
19 The grandchildren could see the diviner and mother's collection of pictures (8)

## Down

1 Attacks fool with a terrible lust (8)
2 Bellow for one of crew after start of race (4)
3 Rats running wildly around in coaches (6)
4 Uniform has a medal to display (4)
5 Offensive about to capture Urban District (4)
6 Desiring energy to enter into story-telling (8)
10 Ex-students injured in maul (6)
12 Is pornography this cheap? (4)
13 An employer some abuse regularly (4)
15 A figure I study carefully (4)

---

### Quizzical Quote

'The little I know, I owe to my ignorance.'

*Sacha Guitry*

---

# GIVE AND TAKE

★★★

Here is a puzzle by Dave Crosland, alias 'Smokey', one of the best crossword compilers we have today.

In half the Across and half the Down clues, the definition contains one letter too many; in the remaining clues, the definition is one letter short. Answers are to be inserted normally.

## Across

1 I'm getting high, reversing in taxi (5)
4 Flan provides a scrap to eat during evening meal (9)
9 Reside touching the sea, one that's receding (9)
10 Journalist for a day is crooked (5)
11 Violently resists ladies in wars (7)
12 Drop of rum in tumbler makes you waver (7)
13 Medal dad's got in retirement (6)
15 Is frightened to swallow the plums (8)
18 With freight loaded in, casually set sail (8)
20 Save donkey caught by Irish singer (6)
23 Replace president: he's to be restored during alert (7)
24 Master-stroke allowed win (7)
26 Sallow king has lost his second (5)
27 Family taken in by preacher, one with famous lawn (9)
28 With peculiar shape, one no-trump's leading to game-bids (9)
29 Greek 'orse trough (5)

## Down

1 At home, substitute player stormed away (2,7)
2 Chats young Samuel up the wrong way (5)
3 Bogus T. S. Eliot novel (7)
4 One who's fond of Spain is unusually staid after appearance of sun (6)
5 Tories having afterthought about certain kind of farmland (8)
6 Drum away with rhythm (7)
7 Ills to evade: what a good idea (9)
8 Cause is clear, but hesitation ensues (5)
14 Amount of sticky rock with odd shape (4,5)
16 Trouble with chair? Spends about a pound on it (5,4)
17 Plan word-play by ex-PM (8)
19 They rub up King's rings (7)
21 Cosmic swirling of endlessly magic sun (7)
22 One famous for lying sheltered by vicar usually (6)
23 Quip made by wanton, out of bed (3,2)
25 Rita is a girl with nothing on (5)

This ingenious and tantalizing puzzle was created by 'Duck' (which is the pseudonym used by Donald Manley, one of Britain's top crossword compilers).

Clues are normal but each solution is to be coded in one of two ways – either by taking the next letters in the alphabet or taking the ones before (A follows Z). Thus FAG is entered as either GBH or EZF, and EZF could also be the code for DYE (the other possibility being CXD). Half the words are coded 'forward' and half coded 'backward'. Solvers must decide which code applies to each clue.

## Across

1 An academic schedule possibly including a bit of Oratory – something learnt about in English Language? (12)
9 Greek vehicle provided without front and rear lights (6)
10 School recruits? Provide bit of 'elp, a crib almost (6)
12 Passages in which cunning little nuisance is cut short (6)
14 Scribe's old case – names entertained by Lord (6)
15 Seasoning put back in stone cask (6)
16 Christian society containing 'acceptable' and 'unacceptable' people (4)
18 Devious-sounding friend of Peter? (5)
19 One can't adjust if returning in slight fog (6)
20 Former England footballer's short protection for shin (6)
25 Take in the medic's liquid, coloured (5)
29 Creative power grips unknown yeoman (4)
30 Rose is mounted in wax (6)
31 Grain by Fenland canal – you see through it (6)
32 Fashion not English, American – something designed for 'groovy' settings (6)
33 African millet required for Malayan hopper (6)
34 Wood with black reptile crawling endlessly around (6)
35 This plant is kept indoors – winds are able to get at one dreadfully (12)

## Down

1 Quip from wit – rich react violently (12)
2 A purge revolutionized it (6)
3 G-gym? Youngster getting round it played truant in Scotland (6)
4 Indian pagan showing sentimentality about brief study of insects (6)
5 I may be in basket before start of dinner (5)
6 Old shrubs, brown, stunted, dry up (6)
7 Eastern fruit came down on Greek character (6)
8 In the manner of some philosophers I cycle etc. all haywire (12)
11 Old drunkard sent hurtling e.g. rises (6)
13 Squat heap (4)
17 Vessel on river – made by Japanese craftsmen (6)
21 Make good bent copper rope (6)
22 Organized defence around busy centre is slashed (6)
23 Kaffir 'olds steer up (4)
24 Wife of hero brings male child before one (6)
26 Borough with small light metal gate (6)
27 Sort of condenser requiring inductance that's large (6)
28 Heavenly body showing up after 5 (start of evening)? (5)

Stephen Sondheim is world-famous as a song-writer. Not so many people know that he is also a first-class compiler of crossword puzzles.

This puzzle by Sondheim, first published in the *New York Magazine*, is an excellent example of the type of crossword in which the clues are embedded in a narrative – in this case, with an added twist.

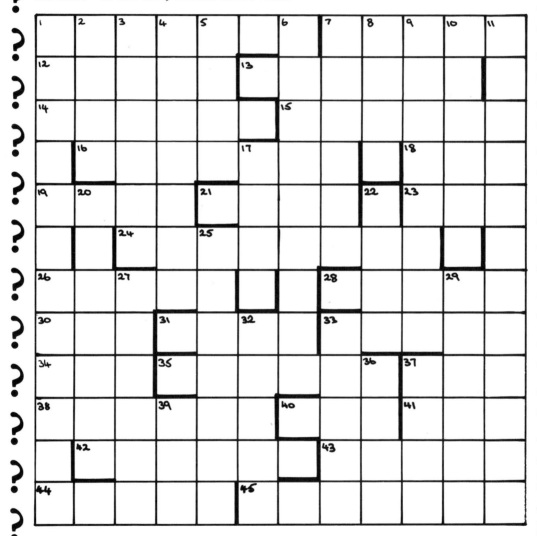

'I **40A** (3) we're **39D** (3) here,' said the Inspector. He was standing in the jungle-like **1D** (12) of the **6D** (9) of the late Sir Leonard Feisthill, **19A** (4) while adviser to the Secret Service Department of **11D** (12) and setter of the weekly crosswords in its house organ, *The Secret Service* **3D** (6). He was speaking to Lucius

I. Feisthill, the deceased's nephew, Dr Nathanael Parmenter, his medical adviser, and **37A** (3) LaFollette, his secretary: 'Last week we had a **18A** (3) that Sir Leonard was about to denounce someone close to him for selling state secrets to the **33D** (5). His **35A** (6) was to publish the traitor's name – in **21A** (4), perhaps – as a warning to the betrayer to cease his nefarious activities. But it looks as if he was **13A** (6) at his own game, for here he lies, **2D** (4) in the back. I suggest we step into the study, where the victim's flight from the murderer began, to **40A** (3) if his desk will **44A** (5) us further clues.' None of the suspects dared **5D** (4) the suggestion and they **39D** (3) followed him, walking carefully around Sir Leonard's **1A** (7).

The walls of the study were lined with books on classical antiquities, Sir Leonard's only reading **7D** (6). (Hidden behind some of them was his famous collection of pornographic one-**20D** (7).) Among the **38A** (6) furnishings (Sir Leonard was a devotee of the decorative **37D** (4) and **25D** (7) on nothing) was a large African desk, acquired in the **26A** (5). On it were a glass of **30A** (3), his well-thumbed copy of the **45A** (7), his rusty typewriter, a thin **16A** (7) of ferric **12A** (5) all over it, and the crossword reprinted on this page, which was to be published the following week. The only other **8D** (4) was an unfinished pencilled work-sheet of Clues for it, as follows:

> Gun Bogart might have used in 'Born to Say No'
> Stare and see parts of the mosaic!
> Alternative finish for a Biblical witch? Quite the reverse!
> Call for help gets nothing for fair.
> Plan in retrospect to help if you put on weight.

'A four-letter, five-letter, six-letter, seven-letter and an eight-letter word,' murmured the Inspector, no **29D** (6) at puzzles himself. 'Odd . . . well, no **7D** (6).' In the **42A** (6) room, **39D** (3) that could be heard was a ladylike **22D** (4) from **37A** (3) and the rasp of a **43A** (5). The Inspector lit his pipe and suddenly turned.

'Miss LaFollette, Sir Leonard had a reputation for being quite a **41A** (3). How well did you know him?'

'Quite well,' the **32D** (5) replied. 'We first met **34A** (3) years ago at one of those literary **36D** (4). **10D** (6) summer it was, I remember, the trees all gold—

'Her favourite colour,' sneered Lucius, trying to **7A** (5) her innocent tone.

'In your **23A** (3), you **9D** (8)!' she screamed – inaccurately, for Lucius was by no means stupid.

'**15A** (6) on,' the Inspector cautioned.

'**37A** (3) is right,' the Doctor put in with his characteristic Vermont **28A** (5). 'I was treating **27D** (6) for a ruptured **31A** (4) at the time – he had chronic trouble with his back.'

'But not with his head,' mused the Inspector. 'Sir Leonard was a man who **4D** (7) himself quickly to any situation and I'm convinced that somewhere in this puzzle is an indication of the murderer's identity, made perhaps even in his presence but too subtle for him to **40A** (3) and therefore destroy.' He gave the puzzle and Clues a moment's study, then whistled softly in realization. 'Now I **40A** (3),' he said, and promptly arrested one of the people in the room.

Whom did he arrest, and what was Sir Leonard's method of accusation?

This cryptic crossword was compiled by Sir Max Beerbohm. It appeared in *The Times* in 1940.

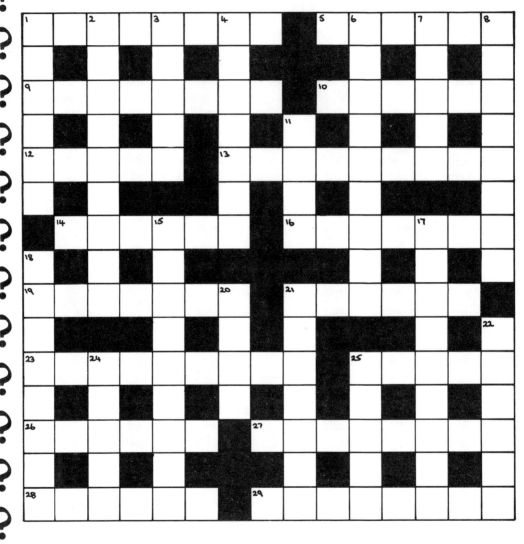

## Across

1 A Victorian statesman lurking in a side lair (8)
5 Milky way unseen by star-gazers (6)
9 An insect with a girl on each side (8)
10 Pugilists' wear (6)
11 Four toes are broken (8)
12 The cockney's goddess appears to have been a slimmer (6)
14 There's a little company in the meadow next month (10)
18 'But what if memory Itself our ———s had betrayed?' (Matthew Arnold) (two words) (5,5)
22 A nudist's aunt? (6)
23 'That day he ——— the Nervii' (Shakespeare) (8)
24 Acknowledgement of debt in a vessel (6)
25 Neither animal nor mineral, and only three-fourths vegetable (8)
26 Not what the wicket-keeper tries for in Essex (6)
27 The PRA is utterly confounded (8)

## Down

1 Drum (Newbolt) (6)
2 The top of the morning, perhaps (6)
3 A Manx beverage (6)
4 Ho! Let's go in (anag.) (10)
6 Wordsworth's fan mail? (8)
7 And yet sugar *can* be refined (8)
8 They are up and doing, no doubt, in 'the sweet o' the year' (8)
13 Little Tommy thought it meant a red-faced blacksmith (10)
15 Voltaire's *prêtre enragé* (8)
16 Such buns are eaten on a good day (two words) (3,5)
17 Caliban's sea-change (8)
19 Pollarded haven (6)
20 I'm in the old Roman bath (6)
21 'Our ——— clues that do but darken counsel' (Tennyson) (6)

# CROSSWORD VARIANTS

To round off this chapter, we present a small selection of puzzles which may be regarded as crossword variants.

## 244
## CROSS-REFERENCE ★★

A Cross-Reference puzzle resembles a crossword, but there are no clues. Instead the letters of the solution are represented by the numbers 1 to 26. Each number always represents the same letter wherever it occurs in the diagram, and all 26 letters of the alphabet are used.

   To give you a start, three letters are identified for you. When you have entered these letters into the diagram wherever their corresponding numbers occur, you should be able to work out the letters represented by one or two other numbers. These letters when they have been entered will enable you to deduce other letters, and so on, until you have completed the puzzle.

| 1 | 2 | 3 | 4 | 5 | 6 | ■ | 7 | 8 | 1 | 9 | 4 | 10 | 11 |
|---|---|---|---|---|---|---|---|---|---|---|---|----|----|
| 2 | ■ | 16 | ■ | 12 | ■ | 13 | ■ | 16 | ■ | 14 | ■ | 17 | 12 |
| 4 | 14 | 5 | 12 | 4 | 13 | 25 | 4 | 10 | ■ | 8 | 1 | 21 | 4 | 10 |
| 8 | ■ | 18 | ■ | 11 | ■ | 16 | ■ | 26 | ■ | 19 | ■ | 19 | ■ | 19 |
| 19 | 17 | 11 | 4 | 6 | ■ | 10 | 16 | 19 | 17 | 22 | 10 | 1 | 1 | 7 |
| 11 | ■ | ■ | ■ | 17 | ■ | 6 | ■ | 17 | ■ | ■ | 25 | ■ | 6 |
| 18 | 19 | 2 | 2 | 25 | 6 | 23 | ■ | 20 | 10 | 16 | 11 | 11 | 24 |
| ■ | 16 | ■ | ■ | 6 | ■ | ■ | ■ | ■ | ■ | 15 | ■ | 8 |
| 16 | 26 | 25 | 11 | 4 | 15 | ■ | 6 | 17 | 3 | 1 | 24 | 4 | 15 |
| 26 | ■ | 2 | ■ | ■ | 16 | ■ | 17 | ■ | 1 | ■ | ■ | 4 |
| 16 | 21 | 1 | 19 | 15 | 16 | 17 | 5 | 4 | ■ | 25 | 17 | 6 | 19 | 8 |
| 24 | ■ | 1 | ■ | 10 | ■ | 20 | ■ | 10 | ■ | 10 | ■ | 10 | ■ | 16 |
| 7 | 19 | 23 | 23 | 24 | ■ | 8 | 4 | 20 | 4 | 17 | 15 | 16 | 10 | 24 |
| 8 | ■ | 8 | ■ | 16 | ■ | 4 | ■ | 24 | ■ | 4 | ■ | 9 | ■ | 4 |
| 24 | 19 | 4 | 8 | 15 | 4 | 15 | ■ | 16 | 15 | 15 | 8 | 4 | 15 |

| 1 | 2 | 3 | 4 | 5 | 6 | 7 | 8 | 9 | 10 | 11 | 12 | 13 |
|---|---|---|---|---|---|---|---|---|----|----|----|----|
| 14 | 15 D | 16 A | 17 N | 18 | 19 | 20 | 21 | 22 | 23 | 24 | 25 | 26 |

To solve this puzzle, the letters which form the answer to each clue have to be eliminated from that line. Every answer contains at least five letters.

Each letter in the diagram forms part of the answer to *either* an across clue *or* a down clue. Therefore once eliminated a letter may not be reused, and all the letters must be eliminated to complete the puzzle.

|    | 1 | 2 | 3 | 4 | 5 | 6 | 7 | 8 | 9 | 10 | 11 | 12 | 13 |
|----|---|---|---|---|---|---|---|---|---|----|----|----|----|
| 1  | S | B | P | N | O | R | N | E | T | O  | H  | I  | P  |
| 2  | O | M | H | E | U | A | O | S | A | D  | I  | U  | N  |
| 3  | G | D | E | A | T | O | T | U | I | A  | N  | R  | B  |
| 4  | L | E | E | G | I | T | C | T | R | O  | S  | H  | U  |
| 5  | E | S | R | I | A | E | L | B | O | F  | B  | P  | T  |
| 6  | W | A | N | J | N | D | E | G | Y | L  | P  | R  | O  |
| 7  | G | U | Y | T | I | N | F | M | A | R  | N  | E  | O  |
| 8  | N | U | E | R | O | M | I | Y | C | G  | U  | A  | V  |
| 9  | A | Z | A | E | J | I | Y | U | H | R  | P  | O  | C  |
| 10 | E | I | O | R | L | G | N | Q | O | R  | G  | A  | U  |
| 11 | D | E | B | A | R | D | U | O | I | Y  | F  | N  | M  |
| 12 | M | A | P | Y | O | T | R | H | U | I  | N  | C  | L  |
| 13 | U | O | M | S | D | Y | W | E | L | N  | O  | L  | I  |

| | *Across* | | | | *Down* | | |
|---|---|---|---|---|---|---|---|
| 1 | Contrary | 8 | Traveller | 1 | Female | 8 | Boiled sweet |
| 2 | Loss of memory | 9 | Soft breeze | 2 | Doubtful | 9 | Pigment |
| 3 | Area | 10 | Argument | 3 | Unison | 10 | Newspaper |
| 4 | Outline | 11 | Taboo | 4 | Deny | 11 | Branch |
| 5 | Swift | 12 | Benefactor | 5 | Pleasure trip | 12 | Pair |
| 6 | Danger | 13 | Single | 6 | Dirty | 13 | Scale |
| 7 | Uninformed | | | 7 | Operate | | |

Each cryptic clue refers to the name of a town or city in England. These words are all hidden in the diagram. They may go up, down, forwards, backwards or diagonally, but always in a straight line. Not all the letters in the diagram will be used, but some are used more than once. Ring the words as you find them.

Solve the clues and then locate the words in the diagram. Or locate the words and then match them up with the clues. It's fun either way!

|    | a | b | c | d | e | f | g | h | i | j | k | l | m | n | o |
|----|---|---|---|---|---|---|---|---|---|---|---|---|---|---|---|
| 1  | Y | K | E | I | L | F | R | O | N | T | O | T | N | E | S |
| 2  | G | M | E | L | M | E | L | S | R | U | B | B | A | T | O |
| 3  | Y | M | N | F | P | L | R | E | T | S | A | C | N | A | L |
| 4  | E | J | O | O | R | A | C | D | E | R | B | O | L | G | D |
| 5  | B | P | T | R | Y | D | T | I | L | T | T | B | J | S | H |
| 6  | L | U | S | D | E | H | D | S | H | G | W | N | T | M | A |
| 7  | Y | C | E | O | D | C | N | C | N | Y | K | O | W | A | M |
| 8  | T | D | K | L | M | O | A | I | R | R | K | D | O | R | L |
| 9  | H | I | L | V | U | R | L | M | A | E | A | R | O | D | L |
| 10 | T | S | O | U | L | R | R | W | B | E | V | B | O | L | E |
| 11 | U | F | F | I | A | W | E | C | H | E | J | O | A | Y | W |
| 12 | R | M | S | D | L | N | D | E | R | U | N | S | D | L | E |
| 13 | D | L | M | A | H | C | N | I | R | T | L | A | N | R | K |
| 14 | E | B | E | J | Y | I | U | S | T | A | R | L | N | C | A |
| 15 | R | D | R | U | M | O | S | C | W | O | R | R | A | J | B |

1. The timber trade (4)
2. Naval base (4)
3. Heart of boy or kid (4)
4. Roved around (5)
5. Feed the furnace (5)
6. Translated poems (5)
7. Sounding happy (5)
8. Fresh boat (6)
9. No test revision (6)
10. Colourful transport (6)
11. Florid characters (6)
12. Stale meat (6)
13. Line of containers (6)
14. Unruly cupids (6)
15. Socialist girl (7)
16. Laws broken by everyone (7)
17. Disturbed slumber (7)
18. Be a good cook (8)
19. Colliery boss (8)
20. Transport material (8)
21. Hold race in ruins (8)
22. No entry for ewes (8)
23. Timber for ships? (9)
24. Ancestral ruins (9)
25. Wise partner (9)
26. What holds a farm building together? (10)
27. Sort of Latin charm (10)
28. Pet heavyweight (10)
29. Separate country (10)
30. People seen to reform (10)

---

**Quizzical Quote**

'If I don't know I don't know, I think I know.
If I don't know I know, I think I don't know.'

*R. D. Laing*

---

109

# HONEYCOMB

★★★

The answers to the clues are all six-letter words. Enter each answer clockwise around the appropriate numbered cell, starting in the cell indicated by the arrow.

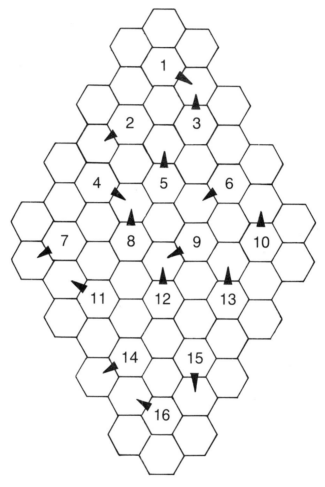

| | |
|---|---|
| 1 Shooting star | 9 Noiseless |
| 2 Choral compositions | 10 Royal seat |
| 3 Very small | 11 Make up one's mind |
| 4 Hymns | 12 Not moving |
| 5 Garden flowers | 13 Sweet made with almonds etc. |
| 6 Crescent-shaped | 14 Journalistic supervisor |
| 7 Stopped | 15 Second childhood |
| 8 A constellation | 16 Gnawing mammal |

# 7.

# LOGIC PUZZLES

## 248
### UP AND DOWN ★★

A boy called Richard lives on the eighteenth floor in a tall block of flats. Whenever he goes to school, he gets into the lift, gets out on the ground floor and walks to school. Whenever he returns, he gets into the lift, goes up to the fifteenth floor, and then walks up three flights of stairs to the eighteenth floor.

Why does he always get out at the fifteenth floor instead of the eighteenth?

## 249
### BEAR FACTS ★★

An explorer left his camp and went due south in a straight line for one mile. Then he turned and walked due east in a straight line for one mile. There, after seeing a bear, he turned and walked due north in a straight line for one mile, which took him back to his camp.

What colour was the bear?

## 250
### EIGHT COINS ★★

You have nine identical-looking coins. One of them is a counterfeit, and the only way of detecting it is by the fact that it is lighter than the genuine coins. The only scale available is a simple balance, without any weights.

Using the scale only twice, can you pick out the counterfeit coin?

## 251
### TWENTY-EIGHT DAYS ★★

Some months have thirty days. Some months have thirty-one days. How many months have twenty-eight days?

## 252
## PRO OR ANTI? ★★

You are taking part in a discussion. Someone says to you 'I couldn't disagree with you less.' Is he expressing agreement or disagreement?

## 253
## CONTINUE THE SERIES ★★

Here is a puzzle that relies on pure intuition for its solution – either you see the answer or you don't.
 What are the next two letters in this sequence?

 O, T, T, F, F, S, S, E, ?, ?

## 254
## THREE CARDS ★★

There are three ordinary playing cards in a row. A heart is on the left of a diamond (though not necessarily next to it); a Seven is on the right of a Queen; an Ace is on the left of a spade; a spade is on the left of a diamond.
 What are the three cards?

## 255
## TRUE AND FALSE ★★

Just one of the following statements is true – which one?

 (a)  One of these statements is false.

 (b)  Two of these statements are false.

 (c)  Three of these statements are false.

 (d)  Four of these statements are false.

 (e)  Five of these statements are false.

 (f)  Six of these statements are false.

## 256
## SONG CONTEST ★★

Of the three finalists in the European song contest, Pierre gets more points than the Swiss entrant, but fewer than the singer of 'Non Plus'. Louis gets fewer points than the Belgian entrant. Jean gets more points than the French entrant. The singer of 'C'est La Vie' gets more points than the singer of 'Quelque Chose'.
 Can you give the name, nationality and song title of each entrant in the order in which they were placed?

## 257
### TOSSING A COIN ★★★

Bill and Ben take turns tossing a coin. Whoever gets a head first is the winner. If Bill has the first toss, he obviously has an advantage. But what exactly is the probability that he will win?

## 258
### DAYS IN A DAZE ★★★

When the day before yesterday was referred to as 'the day after tomorrow', the day that was then called 'yesterday' was as far away from the day we now call 'tomorrow' as yesterday is from the day on which we shall now be able to speak of last Monday as 'a week ago yesterday'.

What day is it?

## 259
### TOM, DICK AND HARRY ★★★

Three friends – Tom, Dick and Harry – meet every Sunday lunchtime for a drink at their local pub. On these occasions each man drinks either gin or whisky. Either Tom or Dick drinks whisky, but not both. If Tom drinks whisky, Harry drinks gin. Dick and Harry do not both drink gin.

One of them sometimes drinks gin and sometimes drinks whisky. Which one?

## 260
### FLATMATES ★★★

Sally, Susan and Sharon are flatmates, and each of them frequently borrows clothes or jewellery belonging to the others. When they went to a party recently, each of them wore a necklace belonging to one of their flatmates and earrings belonging to the other.

If the one wearing Sally's earrings was wearing Susan's necklace, who was wearing Sharon's necklace?

---

**Quizzical Quote**

'Contrariwise,' continued Tweedledee, 'if it was so, it might be; and if it were so, it would be; but as it isn't, it ain't. That's logic.'

*Lewis Carroll*

# RIVER-CROSSING PUZZLES

There are many traditional puzzles involving a group of travellers having to cross a river in a small boat. These travellers may, for example, be men with jealous wives or a group of cannibals and missionaries, but there are always some restrictions as to who can safely be left with whom.

These puzzles have a very long history. They appeared frequently in medieval collections of riddles and puzzles. The earliest recorded example of this type of puzzle is in the works of Alcuin of Northumbria, who was born in Yorkshire in 735 and died at Tours in 804, and who sent one of these puzzles to his pupil, the emperor Charlemagne!

## 261
## MISSIONARIES AND CANNIBALS ★★★

Three missionaries and three cannibals had to cross a river in a small boat that would only carry two men at a time. Being acquainted with the peculiar appetites of the cannibals, the missionaries could never allow their companions to be in a majority on either side of the river.

If only one of the missionaries and one of the cannibals was able to row the boat, how did they all manage to get across?

## 262
## THREE JEALOUS HUSBANDS ★★★

This puzzle was posed by Charles Hutton, in 1803, in his book *Recreations in Mathematics and Natural Philosophy*, but is actually a translation of an earlier puzzle in a French collection published in 1612.

Three jealous husbands with their wives, having to cross a river at a ferry, find a boat without a boatman; but the boat is so small that it can contain no more than two of them at once. How can these six persons cross the river so that no woman shall be left in company with any of the men, unless when her husband is present?

---

### Quizzical Quote

'All modern thought is permeated by the idea of thinking the unthinkable.'

*Michel Foucault*

---

# LIARS AND TRUTH-TELLERS

There are many puzzles, old and new, about a mysterious island on which the natives are divided into two tribes. The members of one tribe always tell the truth, while the members of the other tribe always tell lies.

Many different names have been given to this island, and to the two tribes. No two puzzle composers ever seem to agree on the correct names. To settle this controversy once and for all, I will tell you that the name of the island is Tru-Li, that the tribe of truth-tellers is called the Truis and the tribe of liars is called the Lias.

Of course you will have to take all this with a pinch of salt if you believe that I might be a Lia!

## 263
## THE ISLAND OF TRU-LI – 1     ★★★

A missionary was visiting the island of Tru-Li. Seeing a native in the distance, he said to a nearby native, 'Go and ask that native in the distance whether he is a Trui or a Lia.' When the messenger returned, he replied, 'He says he is a Trui.'

Is the messenger a Trui or a Lia? And what about the native in the distance?

## 264
## THE ISLAND OF TRU-LI – 2     ★★★

The same missionary later encountered two more natives of Tru-Li standing in a jungle clearing. Their names were A and B.

The missionary asked A, 'Are you a Trui or a Lia?' A answered, but the missionary did not hear his reply. So the missionary asked B, 'What did A say?' B replied, 'A said he is a Lia.' A then spoke up, saying, 'No, I didn't. B is lying.'

Can you say whether each of the natives is a Trui or a Lia?

## 265
## THE ISLAND OF TRU-LI – 3     ★★★

The same missionary met a further two natives of Tru-Li, called C and D. C said to the missionary, 'Of the two of us – C and D – at least one is a liar.'

What are C and D?

## 266
## THE ISLAND OF TRU-LI – 4     ★★★

Suppose, in the previous puzzle, both C and D had denied belonging to the same tribe.

What would that have told you about C and D?

## 267
## THE ISLAND OF TRU-LI – 5 ★★★

Our old friend, the missionary on the island of Tru-Li, is on a long journey across the island, and comes to a fork in the road. One road leads to his destination but he is not sure which one it is. There are two natives standing nearby. How, by asking one of the natives only one question, can he find out which of the two roads he should take?

## 268
## A GAME OF WHIST ★★★

Pat, Chris, Lee and Kit are four friends. They seldom meet during the week because their various jobs – journalist, teacher, estate agent, hairdresser – keep them fully occupied. But they meet every Saturday evening for a game of whist.

Last Saturday, when they played, Pat's partner was the journalist, who was seated on Kit's left. Lee partnered the hairdresser.

If I tell you that Chris is neither the journalist nor the estate agent, perhaps you can tell me the occupation of each person.

## 269
## A STRAIGHTFORWARD QUESTION ★★★

If the puzzle you solved before you solved the puzzle after you solved the puzzle you solved before you solved this one was easier than the puzzle you solved after you solved the puzzle you solved before you solved this one, was the puzzle you solved before you solved this one easier than this one?

Yes or no?

## 270
## MARKS FOR LOGIC ★★★

Three men apply for the post of research assistant to a professor of logic. Since all three are equally suitable, the professor announces that he will set them a problem, the job going to the applicant who first solves it correctly.

The professor seats the three applicants in the same room, and puts a mark on each applicant's forehead. The three are told that each has either a red mark or a green mark on his forehead. Each is to raise his hand if he sees a red mark on the forehead of either of the others. The first one to tell correctly the colour of the mark on his own forehead and to explain how he arrived at the answer will get the job.

All three applicants raise their hands. After a little while, one applicant correctly identifies the colour of the mark on his own forehead. What colour was it, and how did he work it out?

## 271
## THE COMMITTEE ★★★

There are four members on the committee – the chairman, vice-chairman, secretary and treasurer. Their names, not necessarily in the same order, are Matthew, Mark, Luke and John.

The chairman and the treasurer are cousins, but Mark and Matthew are not related to each other. The vice-chairman's wife is called Mary, and the secretary's fiancée is called Jane. The secretary is older than both Mark and Matthew. Luke has recently had a disagreement with the treasurer. Matthew and Luke are the only ones who are married.

On the basis of this information, can you assign each man to his right place on the committee?

## 272
## KING ARTHUR'S KNIGHTS ★★★★

King Arthur sat at the Round Table on three successive evenings with his knights – Beleobus, Caradoc, Driam, Eric, Floll and Galahad – but on no occasion did any person have as his neighbour one who had before sat next to him. On the first evening they sat in alphabetical order round the table. But afterwards King Arthur arranged the two next sittings so that he might have Beleobus as near to him as possible and Galahad as far away from him as could be managed. How did he seat the knights to the best advantage, remembering that rule that no knight may have the same neighbour twice?

## 273
## FOUR LADIES ★★★★

Here are four facts about four ladies:

(a) Rose earns more than Miss Christie, who lives exactly six miles from Ivy, who lives directly south of Miss Sayers.

(b) Olive earns more than the research chemist, who lives directly east of Ivy.

(c) The archaeologist earns more than Miss James, and Hazel earns more than the market analyst.

(d) The research chemist lives directly north of Miss Marsh, who lives exactly ten miles from Rose, who lives exactly four miles from the optician.

Which lady earns the most? Which lady is the market analyst? How far apart do Hazel and Olive live?

## A DINNER-PARTY                                    ★★★★

When Mr and Mrs Thompson gave a dinner-party, they invited Mr and Mrs Johnson, Mr and Mrs Edmundson, Mr and Mrs Richardson and Mr and Mrs Stevenson.

The ten people were seated at a circular table, and no man sat next to his own wife. Mr Thompson sat next but one to Mrs Stevenson. Mr Edmundson sat between two ladies, and so did Mr Richardson. Mrs Johnson sat next to her sister, while Mr Johnson sat next but one to Mr Stevenson, who was immediately to the left of his father-in-law. Mrs Edmundson sat next but two to her husband, and Mrs Johnson sat next but two to Mrs Richardson. Three of the ladies each sat between two men.

Can you say in what order the ten people were seated at the table?

## 275
## LEWIS CARROLL'S SYMBOLIC LOGIC – 1                ★★★★

In his book *Symbolic Logic*, Lewis Carroll attempted to make logic entertaining by presenting his readers with a number of puzzles. In these puzzles you are given a number of premises. By taking any pair of premises which have a common term, you can draw a conclusion. Combine this result with another premise which has a common term, and it is possible to draw a new conclusion. If you continue with this process, you will end up with an ultimate conclusion which takes into account all the original premises. This ultimate conclusion will be the same regardless of the order in which you combine the premises.

Now, see what ultimate conclusion you can draw from these premises:

(a)  All the human race, except my footmen, have a certain amount of common-sense;

(b)  No one, who lives on barley-sugar, can be anything but a mere baby;

(c)  None but a hopscotch player knows what real happiness is;

(d)  No mere baby has a grain of common-sense;

(e)  No engine-driver ever plays hopscotch;

(f)  No footman of mine is ignorant of what true happiness is.

## SYMBOLIC LOGIC – 2 ★★★★

What ultimate conclusion can you draw from these premises?

(a) All the dated letters in this room are written on blue paper;

(b) None of them are in black ink, except those that are written in the third person;

(c) I have not filed any of them that I can read;

(d) None of them, that are written on one sheet, are undated;

(e) All of them, that are not crossed, are in black ink;

(f) All of them, written by Brown, begin with 'Dear Sir';

(g) All of them, written on blue paper, are filed;

(h) None of them, written on more than one sheet, are crossed;

(i) None of them, that begin with 'Dear Sir', are written in the third person.

## SYMBOLIC LOGIC – 3 ★★★★

What ultimate conclusion can you draw from these premises?

(a) The only animals in this house are cats;

(b) Every animal is suitable for a pet, that loves to gaze at the moon;

(c) When I detest an animal, I avoid it;

(d) No animals are carnivorous, unless they prowl at night;

(e) No cat fails to kill mice;

(f) No animals ever take to me, except what are in this house;

(g) Kangaroos are not suitable for pets;

(h) None but carnivores kill mice;

(i) I detest animals that do not take to me;

(j) Animals that prowl at night always love to gaze at the moon.

At the beginning of this chapter we had a puzzle in which you had to detect a counterfeit among nine coins. The present puzzle is a much harder variation of that one, and it first appeared during the 1940s.

It is said that this puzzle nearly lost World War II for the Allies, because scientists engaged on vital war work spent so much of their time trying to solve this puzzle instead of concentrating on the work they were supposed to be doing. There was even a serious proposal to inflict equal damage on the German war effort by dropping copies of the puzzle (translated into German) in enemy territory.

Here is the puzzle. You have twelve identical-looking coins, one of which is a counterfeit. The counterfeit is either lighter or heavier than the genuine coins, but you do not know which. To help you find the counterfeit, you have a simple balance with no weights. In three weighings, find the counterfeit coin and determine whether it is light or heavy.

---

### Quizzical Quote

'Sat up last night till 4 a.m. over a tempting problem, sent me from New York, "to find three equal rational right-angled triangles". I found two . . . but could not find three!'

*From the diary of Lewis Carroll*

---

# 8.

---

# ALL SHAPES AND SIZES

---

**HOW MANY TRIANGLES?** ★★

How many triangles are there in this diagram?

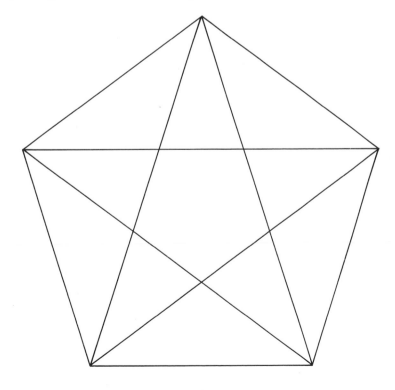

## 280
## A FLOWER BED ★★

In my garden I made a flower bed. If I had made it 2 feet (60 centimetres) wider and 3 feet (1 metre) longer it would have been 63 square feet (5.85 square metres) larger. If I had made it 3 feet (1 metre) wider and 2 feet (60 centimetres) longer it would have been 69 square feet (6.41 square metres) larger.

What are the dimensions of my flower bed?

## 281
## TRACE IT ★★

Can you trace this diagram in one continuous line, without crossing a line, retracing a line, or lifting your pencil from the paper?

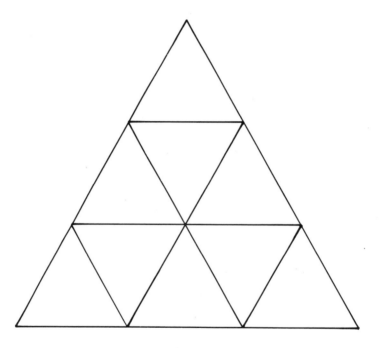

## 282
## THE CARDBOARD BOX ★★

I have a rectangular cardboard box. The top has an area of 240 square inches, the side 300 square inches, and the end 180 square inches.

What are the exact dimensions of the box?

## 283
### HOW LONG IS THE DIAGONAL?                                                    ★★

A rectangle is inscribed in a quadrant of a circle, as shown in the diagram. If the length of AB is 5 and the length of DE is also 5, what is the length of the diagonal AD?

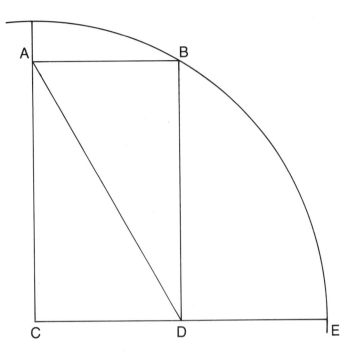

## 284
### THE PAINTED CUBE                                                             ★★

A cube measuring 3 inches (7.62 centimetres) on each side is painted all over, and is then cut into 1-inch (2.54-centimetre) cubes. How many of the small cubes have:

    (a)   paint on three sides?

    (b)   paint on two sides only?

    (c)   paint on one side only?

    (d)   no paint?

## 285
### HOW TO DRAW AN OVAL                                                          ★★

Can you think of an easy way to draw a perfect oval on a sheet of paper with one sweep of the compasses?

## 286
### A SPHERICAL BALLOON ★★

The surface area of a spherical balloon, measured in square inches (centimetres), is the same as its volume, measured in cubic inches (centimetres). What is the diameter of the balloon?

## 287
### BUYING ASPARAGUS ★★

A lady usually buys from her greengrocer large bundles of asparagus, each twelve inches (thirty centimetres) in circumference. The other day the man had no large bundles in stock, but handed her instead two small ones, each six inches (fifteen centimetres) in circumference. 'That is the same quantity,' she said, 'and, of course, the price will be the same.' But the man insisted that the two bundles together contained more than the large one, and charged a little bit extra.

Who was correct – the lady or the greengrocer?

## 288
### CUTTING A RING ★★★

Into how many pieces can you cut this ring shape with three straight cuts. You are not allowed to rearrange the pieces between cuts.

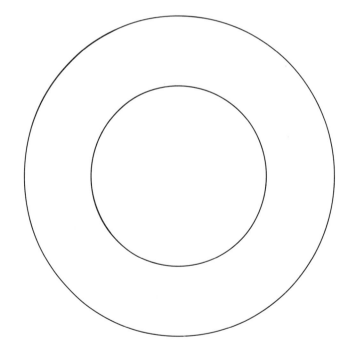

### 289
### THE ARTIST'S CANVAS ★★★

An artist wants to obtain a canvas for a painting which will allow for the picture itself occupying 72 square inches (764 square centimetres), with a margin of 4 inches (10 centimetres) at top and at bottom and 2 inches (5 centimetres) at each side.

What are the smallest dimensions possible for such a canvas?

### 290
### THE LADDER ★★★

A ladder was fastened on end against a high vertical wall. A man unfastened it and pulled it out 11 feet (3.4 metres) at the bottom. It was then found that the top of the ladder had descended one-fifth of the length of the ladder.

What was the length of the ladder?

### 291
### SPHERES ROUND A SPHERE ★★★

A sphere is placed on level ground. How many other spheres of the same size can be placed around it so that they all touch the centre sphere?

### 292
### THE CLOTHES-LINE PUZZLE ★★★

In my garden I have two posts, one 5 feet (1.5 metres) high and the other 7 feet (2.1 metres) high. I tie a clothes-line from the top of each pole to the base of the other.

What is the height from the ground where the two clothes-lines cross?

### 293
### A TANK PUZZLE ★★★

The area of the floor of a tank is 6 square feet (0.55 square metres), and the water in it is 9 inches (23 centimetres) deep. How much does the water rise if a 1-foot (30-centimetre) metal cube is placed in it? How much further does the water rise if a second identical cube is put in alongside the first one?

---

**Quizzical Quote**

'How can I know what I think till I see what I say?'

*Anon.*

---

## STEALING THE BELL-ROPES                                    ★★★

Here is a classic by the Puzzle King, H. E. Dudeney.

Two men broke into a church tower one night to steal the bell-ropes. The two ropes passed through holes in the wooden ceiling high above them, and they lost no time in climbing to the top. Then one man drew his knife and cut the rope above his head, in consequence of which he fell to the floor and was badly injured. His fellow-thief called out that it served him right for being such a fool. He said that he should have done as he was doing, upon which he cut the rope below the place at which he held on. Then, to his dismay, he found that he was in no better plight, for, after hanging on as long as his strength lasted, he was compelled to let go and fall beside his comrade. Here they were both found the next morning with their limbs broken. How far did they fall? One of the ropes when they found it was just touching the floor, and when you pulled the end to the wall, keeping the rope taut, it touched a point just three inches (seven centimetres) above the floor, and the wall was four feet (1.2 metres) from the rope when it hung at rest. How long was the rope from floor to ceiling?

# DISSECTION PUZZLES

In a Dissection Puzzle one has to convert one geometric figure to another by cutting the first into a number of pieces that may be rearranged to form the second.

Puzzles of this type were known to the Chinese several thousand years before the Christian era, and were used as a means of teaching the principles of geometry.

In ancient Greece, a dissection in which a square is transformed into two smaller, unequal squares was used as one proof of the theorem of Pythagoras – that the square on the hypotenuse of a right-angled triangle is equal to the sum of the squares on the other two sides.

Two of the most notable practitioners in this field of puzzledom, at the end of the last century and the beginning of this, were Sam Loyd and H. E. Dudeney. The acknowledged modern master of Dissection Puzzles is an Australian – Harry Lindgren, an examiner for the patent office in Canberra.

## RECTANGLE TO SQUARE – 1                                    ★★

Draw on a piece of cardboard a 9 by 4 rectangle. Cut it into two pieces that may be arranged to form a square. The cut does not need to be a straight-line cut.

# RECTANGLE TO SQUARE – 2 ★★

If you have solved the previous puzzle, you should not have much difficulty with this.

Draw on a piece of cardboard a 16 by 9 rectangle. Cut it into two pieces that may be arranged to form a square. As before, the cut does not need to be a straight-line cut.

## 297
# RECTANGLE TO SQUARE – 3 ★★★

Draw on a piece of cardboard a 5 by 1 rectangle. With four straight-line cuts, divide it into five pieces that can be arranged to form a square.

## 298
# TWO SQUARES TO ONE ★★★

On a piece of cardboard draw a figure similar to that shown, consisting of two squares of different sizes, side by side. The ratio between the sizes of the squares is not important.

Divide this figure by two straight lines to make three parts that can be arranged to form a single perfect square.

## 299
## A GREEK CROSS DISSECTION ★★★

Draw this Greek cross on a piece of cardboard. Then, with two cuts, divide it into four pieces that can be rearranged to form a square.

## 300
## SQUARE TO GREEK CROSSES ★★★

Cut a square into five pieces that will form two separate Greek crosses of different sizes.

### 301
### QUADRUPLICATION

***

Cut out of a piece of cardboard a figure similar to that shown here. The proportions are simply those of a square attached to half of another similar square bisected diagonally.

The puzzle is to cut it into four pieces all of precisely the same size and shape.

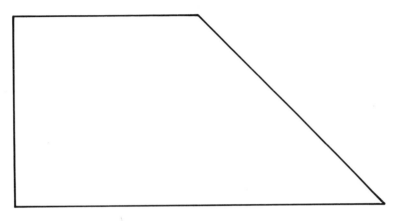

### 302
### THE SPHINX

***

The geometrical figure shown here represents 'The Sphinx'. Can you divide this figure into four similar shaped sphinxes, each one a miniature of the whole, and each of the four parts equal in size?

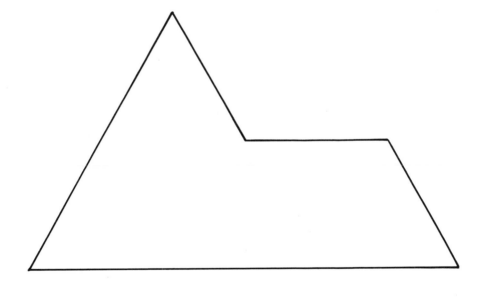

## 303
## TWO FIELDS
**★★★★**

A farmer has two fields. One field is rectangular, exactly twice as long as it is wide. The other field is a perfect square. All the sides of both fields are a whole number of yards (metres).

Although the perimeter of the rectangular field is 816 yards greater than the perimeter of the square field, its area is exactly 1 square yard less than the area of the square field.

What are the dimensions of the two fields?

## 304
## THE SEMI-CIRCULAR ISLAND
**★★★★**

There is a little-known Pacific island which is perfectly semi-circular in shape. Two men start walking from a point on the diameter, one walking along the diameter and the other at right angles to it. The former arrives at the extremity of the diameter after walking 4 miles (6.4 kilometres); the latter reaches the edge of the island after walking 8 miles (13 kilometres).

What is the area of the island?

## 305
## A UNIQUE SPHERE
**★★★★**

The area of a certain sphere is a four-digit integer times *pi*. The volume of the sphere is also a four-digit integer times *pi*.

What is the radius of the sphere (*note*: r is an integer)?

## 306
## COUNTING THE RECTANGLES
**★★★★**

Can you say correctly just how many squares and other rectangles are contained on a chessboard. In other words, in how many ways is it possible to indicate a square or other rectangle enclosed by lines that separate the 64 unit squares?

## 307
## A ROUND-THE-WORLD WALK
**★★★★**

Assuming that you are six feet (1.8 metres) tall, and assuming that the circumference of the earth is 25,000 miles (40,233 kilometres), and assuming that you walk once around the world along the equator, how much further would your head travel than your feet?

---

### Quizzical Quote

'Cudgel thy brains no more about it.'

*Shakespeare: Hamlet*

---

## The Bridges of Konigsberg

That branch of mathematics called topology is concerned with geometric questions in which the size and shape of the figures concerned are irrelevant. The figure may be bent or stretched without affecting the essential nature of the problem.

Topology actually originated with a problem that was proposed by the mathematician Euler. This problem concerned the seven bridges over the River Preger at a place called Konigsberg. The layout of the bridges looked something like this:

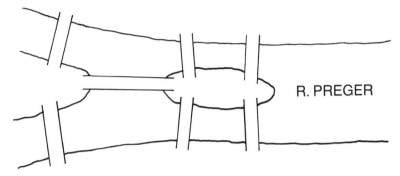

The question was: Is it possible to plan a route so that you pass just once over each of the bridges?

Euler showed that by reducing the areas of land to points and by reducing the bridges to lines, the diagram above is equivalent to this:

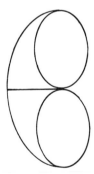

It is impossible to trace a continuous route on this sort of diagram if there are more than two odd nodes – that is, points where an odd number of lines meet. In this case, there are four odd nodes, so it is not possible, in a continuous journey, to pass over each of the Konigsberg bridges just once.

This principle discovered by Euler, and which was the origin of topology, is the same principle that is involved in the sort of puzzle where you have to trace a diagram without lifting your pencil from the paper.

# 9.

---

# QUIZZICAL CHALLENGES

---

**SHOWBIZ**                                                                    ★★

Can you identify these show-business personalities from the brief details given?

(a) He sang with the Tommy Dorsey band. Actor and dancer, as well as a very popular singer, he has appeared in many films, including a series of films in which he played a tough detective.

(b) A British singer and comedienne who made several films. She retired to the isle of Capri. She was made a Dame in 1978.

(c) This British actor, playwright, songwriter and director began his career as a child actor before the First World War. He took the leading role in many of his own plays and shows, and his name was a byword for sophisticated elegance. He wrote the script for a famous wartime film. He was knighted in 1970.

(d) An American actor, successful on Broadway before he entered films. His early films include *A Streetcar Named Desire*, *Viva Zapata*, *On The Waterfront* and *Guys and Dolls*.

(e) A British film director who went to work in Hollywood. He was a master of suspense. His 'trademark' was to appear briefly in each of his films.

(f) This actor was a cult figure, although he starred in only three films. He was killed driving his sports car at over 100 miles an hour (161 kilometres an hour).

## 309
## CRIMINAL CONNECTIONS ★★

Can you name the authors who created the following characters?

| | |
|---|---|
| (a) James Bond | (f) Philip Marlowe |
| (b) Father Brown | (g) Hercule Poirot |
| (c) Adam Dalgleish | (h) The Saint |
| (d) Sherlock Holmes | (i) George Smiley |
| (e) Jules Maigret | (j) Lord Peter Wimsey |

## 310
## THE YOUNG ONES ★★

What is the correct word for the young of each of these creatures?

| | |
|---|---|
| (a) Fox | (f) Eel |
| (b) Goose | (g) Seal |
| (c) Deer | (h) Elephant |
| (d) Goat | (i) Hare |
| (e) Swan | (j) Pigeon |

## 311
## MONEY, MONEY, MONEY ★★

Can you name the six European countries whose units of currency are listed here?

| | |
|---|---|
| (a) Drachma | (d) Schilling |
| (b) Peseta | (e) Escudo |
| (c) Dinar | (f) Punt |

## 312
## WHAT THE DICKENS? ★★

In which books by Charles Dickens do the following characters appear?

| | |
|---|---|
| (a) Uriah Heep | (d) Bill Sikes |
| (b) Sidney Carton | (e) Sarah Gamp |
| (c) Augustus Snodgrass | (f) The Infant Phenomenon |

## 313
### GILBERT AND SULLIVAN ★★★

Can you supply the missing words to complete these quotes from Gilbert and Sullivan operas?

(a) 'A wandering minstrel I –
A thing of ****** and *******'

(b) 'Three little ***** from ****** are we'

(c) 'On a cloth untrue
With a twisted cue
And ********** ******** *****'

(d) 'I am the very model of a ****** *****-*******'

(e) 'When ************ duty's to be done,
The *********'s lot is not a happy one'

(f) 'I was a pale young ****** then'

(g) 'So I fell in love with a rich attorney's
******* **** ********'

(h) 'Oh, I am a **** and a ******* bold
And the **** of the Nancy brig'

## 314
### DATES ★★★

What are the dates of the following days?

(a) St Valentine's Day       (d) St Andrew's Day

(b) St George's Day          (e) St David's Day

(c) St Patrick's Day

## 315
### LAND-LOCKED ★★★

Can you name twenty countries that have no coastline?

## 316
### STATES ★★★

Twenty-one states of the USA have names ending with the letter A. How many of them can you name?

## 317
## FIRST NAMES FIRST
***

What are the first names of the following famous artists and composers?

(a) Picasso

(b) Beethoven

(c) Van Gogh

(d) Elgar

(e) Landseer

(f) Mahler

(g) Matisse

(h) Vivaldi

(i) Dürer

(j) Delius

## 318
## OUT OF TOWN
***

How far from London are these towns?

(a) Birmingham – 98, 118 or 138 miles?

(b) Brighton – 33, 43 or 53 miles?

(c) Bristol – 120, 140 or 160 miles?

(d) Carlisle – 207, 257 or 307 miles?

(e) Dover – 58, 78 or 98 miles?

(f) Edinburgh – 365, 405 or 455 miles?

(g) Hereford – 135, 155 or 175 miles?

(h) Inverness – 464, 514 or 564 miles?

(i) Plymouth – 212, 242 or 272 miles?

(j) York – 209, 239 or 269 miles?

---

### Quizzical Quote

'Think! I've got enough to do, and little enough to get for it, without thinking.'

*Charles Dickens*

---

## AUTHORS A TO Z ★★★

Here is a quiz for bookworms. All you have to do is to identify correctly the authors of the following twenty-five novels. Each author's surname begins with a different letter of the alphabet from A to Z (excluding X) but they are not necessarily in sequence.

| | | | |
|---|---|---|---|
| (a) | The Grapes of Wrath | (n) | The Bottle Factory Outing |
| (b) | Animal Farm | (o) | Kane and Abel |
| (c) | Vanity Fair | (p) | Goodbye To Berlin |
| (d) | A Passage To India | (q) | Zorba The Greek |
| (e) | Three Men In A Boat | (r) | Germinal |
| (f) | Around The World In Eighty Days | (s) | Vile Bodies |
| (g) | Doctor Zhivago | (t) | The Roman Hat Mystery |
| (h) | Peyton Place | (u) | Stranger In A Strange Land |
| (i) | The Red Badge Of Courage | (v) | Castle Rackrent |
| (j) | The Ginger Man | (w) | Lord Of The Flies |
| (k) | Portnoy's Complaint | (x) | Pnin |
| (l) | Exodus | (y) | The Foxes Of Harrow |
| (m) | How Green Was My Valley | | |

## FOR LATIN LOVERS ★★★

Latin may be a dead language, but it lives on in many words and expressions that we still use today. Here are twelve Latin phrases that are in current use. Can you say what each of them means?

| | | | |
|---|---|---|---|
| (a) | Compos mentis | (g) | Ultra vires |
| (b) | Sine qua non | (h) | Sine die |
| (c) | Lapsus linguae | (i) | Ex post facto |
| (d) | A fortiori | (j) | Ad rem |
| (e) | Flagrante delicto | (k) | Quid pro quo |
| (f) | Mens sana in corpore sano | (l) | Ipso facto |

## 321
## FEATHERS OR FINS ★★★

To solve this puzzle you have to identify each of these creatures as having either feathers or fins. In other words, is it a bird or is it a fish?

| Bib | Goby | Kite | Pope | Stilt |
|-----|------|------|------|-------|
| Booby | Grebe | Lory | Porgy | Stint |
| Chub | Gurami | Moa | Rail | Towhee |
| Dory | Keta | Ousel | Sprod | Twite |

## 322
## OLD MASTERS ★★★

Can you name the artists who painted the following famous paintings?

(a)   The Laughing Cavalier

(b)   The Hay-wain

(c)   The Night Watch

(d)   The Lace-maker

(e)   Madame Récamier

(f)   La Grande Odalisque

(g)   The Light Of The World

(h)   Nude Descending A Staircase

(i)   A Sunday Afternoon At The Grande Jatte

(j)   The Fighting Téméraire

## 323
## A ROSE BY ANY OTHER NAME ★★★★

Here are the names of several common garden plants. What are their more down-to-earth English names?

| (a) Althaea | (g) Cytisus | (m) Myosotis |
|-------------|-------------|--------------|
| (b) Antirrhinum | (h) Iberis | (n) Nepeta |
| (c) Araucaria | (i) Kniphofia | (o) Papaver |
| (d) Centaurea | (j) Lathyrus | (p) Parthenocissus |
| (e) Colchicum | (k) Lonicera | (q) Salix |
| (f) Crataegus | (l) Muscari | (r) Syringa |

## 324
### SHAKESPEARE'S PEOPLE ★★★★

Here is a list of Shakespearean characters. All you need to do is name the play in which each character appears.

| | | | | | | | |
|---|---|---|---|---|---|---|---|
| (a) | Dull | (d) | Ariel | (g) | Froth | (j) | Nicanor |
| (b) | Eros | (e) | Bagot | (h) | Rugby | (k) | Donalbain |
| (c) | Snug | (f) | Curio | (i) | Mouldy | (l) | Fortinbras |

## 325
### COMPOSERS ★★★★

In the first column is a list of musical works. In the second column is a list of composers. Can you match each work with the correct composer?

| | | |
|---|---|---|
| (a) | The 1812 Overture | Rossini |
| (b) | The Enigma Variations | Sibelius |
| (c) | The Four Seasons | Verdi |
| (d) | Bolero | Borodin |
| (e) | Turandot | Beethoven |
| (f) | Finlandia | Khatchaturian |
| (g) | Eine Kleine Nachtmusik | Tchaikovsky |
| (h) | La Boutique Fantasque | Poulenc |
| (i) | Carnival of the Animals | Smetana |
| (j) | The Pearl Fishers | Ravel |
| (k) | Radetzky March | Orff |
| (l) | Moonlight Sonata | Elgar |
| (m) | La Traviata | Mozart |
| (n) | Scheherazade | Respighi |
| (o) | Gayaneh | Puccini |
| (p) | The Bartered Bride | Saint-Saëns |
| (q) | Prince Igor | Rimsky-Korsakov |
| (r) | The Pines of Rome | Vivaldi |
| (s) | Carmina Burana | Bizet |
| (t) | Les Biches | Strauss |

(a) Roger Bannister is the first man to run a mile (1.6 kilometres) in under four minutes. Food rationing ends in Britain. K2, the world's second highest mountain, is climbed. What's the year?

(b) William I of Prussia becomes Emperor of Germany. The Commune of Paris is proclaimed. Trade Unions are legalized in Britain. What's the year?

(c) Polaris missile agreement is signed by US and Britain. £2½ million is stolen from London–Glasgow mail train. President Kennedy is assassinated. What's the year?

(d) The League of Nations holds its first meeting. Prohibition starts in the USA. The Ottoman Empire is broken up. What year is it?

(e) Penny postage is introduced in Britain. Queen Victoria marries Prince Albert of Saxe-Coburg-Gotha. The Opium War between Britain and China begins. The last convicts arrive in New South Wales. What's the year?

(f) Major Yuri Gagarin makes first successful space flight. South Africa becomes a republic and leaves the Commonwealth. Boy Scouts are allowed to wear long trousers. There is a volcanic eruption on Tristan da Cunha. What's the year?

**327**
**EMINENT PEOPLE** ★★★★

Here is a list of twelve people who were eminent in various fields of endeavour. They were: an actor, a chess player, a pianist, a poet, a film producer, a physicist, a printer, a sculptor, an educational reformer, an architect, a dramatist and a landscape painter. Who was what?

(a) René Clair

(b) Claude Lorrain

(c) William Congreve

(d) Frank Dobson

(e) Johann Gutenberg

(f) Edmund Kean

(g) Emanuel Lasker

(h) Sir Edwin Landseer Lutyens

(i) Hugh McDiarmid

(j) Johann Heinrich Pestalozzi

(k) Max Planck

(l) Artur Schnabel

Each line of verse below is the second line of a well-known poem. What you have to do is give the first line and identify the poet.

(a)    In a beautiful pea-green boat

(b)    That floats on high o'er vales and hills

(c)    Alone and palely loitering?

(d)    And I will pledge with mine

(e)    Thou art more lovely and more temperate

(f)    The lowing herd wind slowly o'er the lea

(g)    Now that April's there

(h)    Of cloudless climes and starry skies

(i)    Bird thou never wert

(j)    Walk upon England's mountains green?

(k)    Awoke one night from a deep dream of peace

(l)    As through an Alpine village passed

(m)   What so proudly we hailed at the twilight's last gleaming

(n)    Half a league onward

(o)    (Capten, art tha sleepin' there below?)

(p)    And a small cabin build there, of clay and wattles made

(q)    Are losing theirs and blaming it on you

(r)    That there's some corner of a foreign field

(s)    And all I ask is a tall ship and a star to steer her by

(t)    Did gyre and gimble in the wabe

---

### Quizzical Quote

'The golden rule is that there are no golden rules.'

*George Bernard Shaw*

---

# QUIZ QUIZ
**★★★★**

Each of these clues is to be answered with one word. Three of the answers begin with the letter Q, three with U, three with I, and three with Z.
   What are the twelve words?

(a)   The monetary unit of Poland.

(b)   A solid with twenty plane faces.

(c)   Nettle-rash.

(d)   Fabulous Javanese tree that poisoned everything over a large surrounding area.

(e)   God of the west wind.

(f)   An arrangement of five things at the corners and centre of a square.

(g)   In Greek mythology, the ethereal juice in the veins of the gods.

(h)   In Norse mythology, the abode of the giants.

(i)   An alkaloid used in medicine and obtained from cinchona bark.

(j)   In chess, a position in which any move is disadvantageous.

(k)   Books printed before the year 1500.

(l)   A long-tailed bird and the unit of currency of Guatemala.

# LISTS
**★★★★★**

Most people should be able to answer one or two of these questions correctly, but if you can answer them all, then general knowledge is obviously your specialist subject.

(a)   List the five Great Lakes of North America.

(b)   List the nine major planets of the solar system.

(c)   List the twelve signs of the zodiac.

(d)   List the Seven Wonders of the Ancient World.

(e)   List the nine Muses of Greek mythology.

(f)   List the seven deadly sins.

(g)   List the twelve months of the French Revolutionary calendar.

(h)   List the kings and queens of Britain since 1660 (in the correct order).

# 10.

# ALLSORTS

### The Big Prize Puzzle Contest

During the Great Depression in the 1930s in America, prize puzzle contests were very popular. Perhaps the greatest of these was the Old Gold Rebus Contest.

On 25 January 1937 the manufacturers of Old Gold cigarettes advertised their contest in 350 newspapers nationwide. They offered a first prize of 100,000 dollars, with another 100,000 dollars to be distributed among 999 runners-up. The contest was to be spread over fifteen weeks with six puzzles to be solved each week. The contestants' weekly entries had to be accompanied by three wrappers from Old Gold cigarettes.

Each puzzle was a cartoon supposed to represent the name of a famous person. The first puzzles were very simple but during the course of the contest they became increasingly obscure and difficult. The reference sections of public libraries were overrun with contestants seeking information to help them solve the puzzles. Many contestants, having found the information they required in a reference book, would tear out the page to prevent the same information falling into the hands of rival contestants.

By the end of the contest, two million hopeful puzzlers had submitted entries – accompanied by 90 million wrappers. Sales of Old Gold cigarettes had increased by 70 per cent. 54,000 entrants had answered all 90 puzzles correctly, so another 90 even more difficult puzzles were set as tie-breakers. Still there were 9000 contestants left in the running. A naval cadet was the lucky winner of the final tie-breaker, in which the contestants had to write an essay on 'The increased popularity of Old Gold cigarettes in my community as a result of the Old Gold contest'.

The contest cost the company 2 million dollars, which included the wages for 1000 temporary clerical staff, and the mailing of entries provided the Post Office with an extra 1 million dollars revenue.

## 331
## JANET AND JOHN ★★

When she is one year older than she is now, Janet will be twice as old as she was two years ago.

When he is one year older than he is now, John will be three times as old as he was three years ago.

How old are Janet and John?

## 332
## WHAT ARE WE? ★★

Twice eight are ten of us, and ten but three;
Three of us are five. What can we be?
If this be not enough, I'll tell you more –
Twelve of us are six, and nine but four.

## 333
## AN ISOSCELES TRIANGLE ★★

One side of an isosceles triangle is 15 inches (38 centimetres). Another side is 7 inches (18 centimetres). What is the length of the third side?

## 334
## COMPLETE THE VERSE ★★

What letter is missing from this piece of verse? How should it read?

DNTBRRWFRMTMRRW

DNWRNGSKNWNSRRW

FLSWHNLYLKFRGLD

CMMNCMFRTSDNTHLD

## 335
## A DRINK PROBLEM ★★

A man bought a bottle of wine, but had no corkscrew. How did he extract the wine from the bottle without pulling out the cork, without making a hole in it, and without breaking or piercing the bottle?

## 336
## THE STRIKING CLOCK ★★

If a clock takes six seconds to strike six o'clock, how many seconds will it take to strike twelve o'clock?

## 337
### CENTIGRADE AND FAHRENHEIT ★★

We all know that 0 degrees Centigrade is the same as 32 degrees Fahrenheit, and 100 degrees Centigrade is the same as 212 degrees Fahrenheit. But what temperature is exactly the same in both Centigrade and Fahrenheit?

## 338
### GET THE POINT? ★★

Can you make sense of the following sentence, by adding the necessary punctuation?

SMITH WHERE JONES HAD HAD HAD HAD HAD HAD HAD

HAD HAD HAD THE EXAMINERS APPROVAL

## 339
### BROTHERS AND SISTERS ★★

In my family each girl has an equal number of brothers and sisters but each boy has twice as many sisters as brothers. How many boys and how many girls are there in my family?

## 340
### A PROBLEM OF TIME ★★

Imagine that just as you hear the town hall clock strike noon, your watch goes berserk. The minute hand falls off and the hour hand moves backwards at three times the speed at which it normally goes forwards. What time is it when the hour hand is on nine and the town hall clock next strikes the hour?

## 341
### SILKWORMS ★★

Here is a new variation on an old favourite.
  One and a half silkworms can eat two and a half mulberry leaves in three and a half minutes. Assuming that it eats constantly at the same rate, how many mulberry leaves will one silkworm eat in a week?

## 342
### A CERTAIN NUMBER ★★

If 92 times a certain number is subtracted from 94 times the same number, the result is 96. What's the number?
  This problem is easier than it appears at first sight.

## 343
### A PUNCTUATION PUZZLE ★★

Can you add punctuation to the words below so as to make some sort of sense?

That that is is that that is not is not is not that it it is

## 344
### JACK AND JILL ★★

Jack and Jill were born on the same day of the same year and they are the children of the same parents yet they are not twins. How is that possible?

## 345
### THE SQUARE MATHEMATICIAN ★★

Augustus de Morgan, the mathematician, who died in 1871, used to boast that he was $x$ years old in the year $x^2$. In what year was he born?

## 346
### A PEACOCK PUZZLE ★★

Alec, Bill and Charles were three neighbouring farmers. Alec had a peacock which, one day, laid an egg in Bill's car while it was parked on Charles's land.

All three men claimed the egg. Alec said it was his because his peacock laid it. Bill said it was his because it was laid in his car. Charles said it was his because it was laid on his land.

To which of the three should the egg rightfully belong?

---

### Rubik's Cube

Rubik's Cube was the puzzle sensation of the early 1980s.

It was actually in 1974 that Ernö Rubik, who was a 29-year-old architectural engineer in Budapest, made his first 'Rubik's Cube'. The original was made of wood, but in 1977 he managed to get a plastic version made, which won a prize at the Budapest International Fair in 1978. The Ideal Toy Company was given world distribution rights, and over the next few years Cube Mania swept the world. Tens of millions of Cubes were sold. Teachers of mathematics used it to demonstrate the principles of group theory, and the Cube found a place in New York's Museum of Modern Art.

Some people could solve Rubik's Cube in times as short as twenty-three seconds. But many of the millions who bought it, I suspect, never did manage to solve it at all. It has been calculated that there are about 4.3 times $10^{19}$ ways to arrange the Cube, of which only one is correct. Working through one arrangement a second would take roughly 1,360,000,000,000 years.

---

## THE GARDENER'S DILEMMA ★★

A gardener was told to plant four shrubs at equal distances from each other. How was he to do it?

## ALL SIXES ★★

See how quickly you can find the smallest integer that, when multiplied by seven, gives a result composed entirely of sixes.

---

### Gas, Water, Electricity

This must be a candidate for the title Most Popular Puzzle In The World. Over the years many millions of people must have spent many, many millions of hours trying to solve it.

On a sheet of paper you draw three boxes. Mark them G, W and E to represent Gas, Water and Electricity. Draw another three boxes to represent Houses and number them 1, 2, 3.

| G | W | E |
|---|---|---|

| 1 | 2 | 3 |
|---|---|---|

What you have to do is to draw lines connecting each of the three houses to each of the three services – gas, water and electricity. The lines must not cross each other or pass through any of the six buildings.

Have a go, and see if you can find a solution. But don't spend too long on it – because, unless you cheat, the puzzle is impossible.

---

## WEIGHTS ★★★

What is the least number of weights which will allow you to weigh any article in whole pounds (kilogrammes) from 1 to 40 pounds (0.5 to 18 kilogrammes)?

Consider the situation (a) if the weights may be placed on only one side of the scale, and (b) if the weights may be placed on both sides of the scale.

### 350
## WATCH WHERE YOU GO ★★★

You are stranded in the desert, and the sun is blazing down on you. Your only chance of safety is to head for the oasis which you know is due south. You have no compass, but you are wearing a wristwatch. How do you find the right direction? (You are in the northern hemisphere.)

# THE PUZZLES OF LEWIS CARROLL

Lewis Carroll (1832–98) is, of course, best known as the creator of the immortal *Alice's Adventures In Wonderland* and *Through the Looking-Glass*. His real name was Charles Lutwidge Dodgson, and for most of his adult life he was a lecturer in mathematics at Christ Church College in Oxford.

He was fond of inventing ingenious toys and gadgets and had an abiding interest in games, paradoxes and puzzles of every kind. Several of his puzzle creations will be found elsewhere in this book (pages 66, 83 and 118–19). Here are another seven of his puzzles, demonstrating his varied range.

### 351
## APPLES ON A WALL ★

Dreaming of apples on a wall,
And dreaming often, dear,
I dreamed that, if I counted all,
– How many would appear?

### 352
## THE MONKEY PUZZLE ★★

A rope is hung over a weightless, frictionless pulley attached to the roof of a building. At one end of the rope is a ten-pound weight which exactly counterbalances a monkey at the other end. What happens to the weight if the monkey attempts to climb the rope?

*I* think this is a very easy puzzle. But not everyone agrees with me. After publishing the puzzle, Carroll recorded in his diary: 'It is very curious, the different views taken by good mathematicians. Price says the weight goes *up*, increasing velocity. Clifton (and Harcourt) that it goes *up*, at the same rate as the monkey, while Sampson says that it goes *down*!' What do *you* think?

## 353
### THE KING'S WISE MEN ★★★

When the King found that his money was nearly all gone, and that he really *must* live more economically, he decided on sending away most of his Wise Men. There were some hundreds of them – very fine old men, and magnificently dressed in green velvet gowns with gold buttons: if they *had* a fault, it was that they always contradicted one another when he asked for their advice – and they certainly ate and drank *enormously*. So, on the whole, he was rather glad to get rid of them. But there was an old law, which he did not dare to disobey, which said that there must always be:

'Seven blind of both eyes:
  Ten blind of one eye:
Five that see with both eyes:
  Nine that see with one eye.'

How many Wise Men did he keep?

## 354
### THREE SONS ★★★

A man has three sons. At first, two of the ages are together equal to the third. A few years afterwards, two of them are together double the third. When the number of years since the first occasion is two-thirds of the sum of the ages on that occasion, one age is 21.

What are the other two ages?

## 355
### A CIRCULAR RAILWAY ★★★

(a) Two travellers, starting at the same time, went opposite ways round a circular railway. Trains start each way every fifteen minutes, the easterly ones going round in three hours, the westerly in two. How many trains did each meet on the way, not counting trains met at the terminus itself?

(b) They went round, as before, each traveller counting as 'one' the train containing the other traveller. How many did each meet?

## 356
### A SPIRAL WALK ★★★

An oblong garden, half a yard (metre) longer than wide, consists entirely of a gravel-walk, spirally arranged, a yard (metre) wide and 3630 yards (3319 metres) long. Find the dimensions of the garden.

THIS STATEMENT IS FALSE

## 357
### THE BASKET ESCAPE    ★★★★

A captive queen and her son and daughter were shut up in the top room of a very high tower. Outside their window was a pulley with a rope round it, and a basket fastened at each end of the rope of equal weight. They managed to escape with the help of this and a weight they found in the room, quite safely. It would have been dangerous for any of them to come down if they weighed more than 15 pounds (6.8 kilogrammes) more than the contents of the lower basket, for they would do so too quickly, and they also managed not to weigh less either.

The one basket coming down would naturally of course draw the other up.

How did they do it?

The queen weighed 195 pounds (88.5 kilogrammes), daughter 105 (47.6), son 90 (40.8), and the weight 75 (34).

## 358
### WHAT'S THE DAY?    ★★★

A hiker, taking a long walk in the countryside, chanced upon a yokel sitting on a stile. He felt convinced that he had chanced upon the village idiot, and decided to test the fellow's intelligence by putting to him the simplest question he could think of: 'What day of the week is this, my good man?'

This is the answer he received: 'When the day after tomorrow is yesterday, today will be as far from Sunday as today was from Sunday when the day before yesterday was tomorrow.'

Now, what *was* the day of the week?

## 359
### TWELVE ROWS    ★★★

An army officer commanded his men to arrange themselves in twelve rows with eleven men in each row, in such a way that he would be equidistant from every row.

If the officer had 120 men, how could his order be carried out?

---

### Quizzical Quote

'Unless you expect the unexpected you will never find truth, for it is hard to discover and hard to attain.'

*Heraclitus*

---

The following lines were written by Arthur Connor, a prominent figure in the Irish Rebellion of 1798. He was arrested, and wrote the verses while in prison. He made his escape to France in 1807, where he became a general in the army.

> The pomps of Courts and pride of kings
> I prize above all earthly things;
> I love my country, but the King,
> Above all men, his praise I sing.
> The Royal banners are displayed,
> And may success the standard aid.

> I fain would banish far from hence
> The 'Rights of Man' and 'Common Sense'.
> Confusion to his odious reign,
> That foe to princes, Thomas Paine.
> Defeat and ruin seize the cause
> Of France, its liberties and laws.

These two apparently loyal verses, if properly read, bear a very different meaning. Can you discover it?

**361**
## TRUE OR BLUFF?
★★★★

All you have to do is say whether the definition given for each word is True or Bluff.

(a) Keddah — an enclosure for catching wild elephants.

(b) Heyduck — a type of brigand.

(c) Conjee — the warden of a castle.

(d) Div — an evil spirit of Persian mythology.

(e) Pygostyle — an ore containing silver.

(f) Cavesson — an instrument resembling a xylophone.

(g) Serdab — a secret chamber in an Egyptian tomb.

(h) Dicynodont — a ridge-sole rock-climbing boot.

(i) Epizeuxis — the immediate repetition of a word for emphasis.

(j) Oxymel — a mixture of vinegar and honey.

## 362
## A VIEW OF THE EARTH ★★★★

At what distance from the earth is it possible to see exactly one-third of the earth's surface?

## 363
## THE ANAGRAM PROGRAM ★★★★

A whizz-kid friend of mine has written a computer program to help him solve crossword puzzles. The program works by asking him to type in a word, and then it prints out all the possible anagrams of that word. The program does not have access to a dictionary, so it does not know which anagrams are valid words – it just prints out every possible arrangement of the letters. It does, however, recognize repeated letters in the word. So if he asks for anagrams of TOP, it will print out five anagrams: TPO, POT, PTO, OPT, OTP. But if he asks for anagrams of ADD, it will only print out two: DAD and DDA.

Now, perhaps you can tell me how many anagrams this program will print out for each of the following words:

(a) STARE          (d) DELETES

(b) CRATER         (e) RESIDENTS

(c) TERRACE        (f) TRESPASSERS

Perhaps you can do something the program can't, and also tell me which valid one-word anagrams (if any) exist for each of these words.

## 364
## THE END OF THE WORLD ★★★★

If the end of the world should come on the first day of a new century, what are the chances that it will happen on a Sunday?

## 365
## COMMANDOS ★★★★★

Two commandos were on the edge of a perpendicular cliff, 300 feet (91.5 metres) high. They wanted to descend to the centre of a field, at a point exactly 1 mile (1.6 kilometre) from the base of the cliff. One commando climbed down the cliff by rope, and then walked straight to the spot. The other ascended, in a helicopter, a certain distance vertically in a straight line, and then headed directly for the centre of the field.

If both commandos travelled exactly the same distance, how high did the helicopter ascend in that perpendicular line?

## A Roman Word-Square

```
R O T A S
O P E R A
T E N E T
A R E P O
S A T O R
```

This remarkable Roman word-square was first discovered while excavations were being done at the site of the Roman city at Cirencester in Gloucestershire. Another example was later found at Pompeii.

The word-square really is remarkable. Not only is it a valid Latin sentence – it may be translated as 'Arepo the sower guides the wheels at work' – but it is also a palindrome, reading the same backwards as it does forwards. The letters may also be arranged in the form of a cross to form this:

```
                    A
                    P
                    A
                    T
                    E
                    R
A P A T E R N O S T E R O
                    O
                    S
                    T
                    E
                    R
                    O
```

Could this be a primitive Latin crossword puzzle?

# SOLUTIONS

## 1
## UP AND DOWN

An umbrella.

## 2
## THE FROG

Twenty-eight hours.

## 3
## INDIANS

The taller one was the shorter one's mother.

## 4
## A CHEMICAL COMPOUND

The letters are H to O, so the compound is water ($H_2O$).

## 5
## AN ANAGRAM

The letters may be arranged to make JUST ONE WORD.

## 6
## SOCKS

If I take out three socks, two of them are sure to make a matching pair.

## 7
## A STRANGE HOUSE

My house must be built at the South Pole.

## 8
## A PUZZLING RHYME

Too wise you are,
Too wise you be.
I see you are
Too wise for me.

## 9
## CIGARETTE ENDS

Eight. He makes seven cigarettes first of all. When he has smoked these, he is left with seven ends with which to make the eighth cigarette.

## 10
## WHICH IS HEAVIER?

They are both the same weight – one pound (kilogram).

## 11
## HOW MANY ANIMALS?

Three – one horse, one sheep and one pig.

## 12
## AN ALARMING PUZZLE

One – the alarm clock went off an hour after I set it.

## 13
## ODD BOOKS

(a)  OLIVER TWIST
(b)  THE TIME MACHINE
(c)  ROBINSON CRUSOE
(d)  WATERSHIP DOWN
(e)  LITTLE WOMEN.

## 14
## HOW OLD IS HOWARD?

Nine.

## 15
## A QUESTION FOR COOKS

In the same way as short ones!

## 16
## FIVE-LETTER ANIMALS

BISON.

## 17
## GEORGE AND MILDRED

Ten – George, Mildred, their seven daughters and their son.

## 18
## AGES

Cyril is the oldest and Basil is the youngest.

## 19
## EGG TIMERS

He sets both timers going at the same moment. When the three-minute timer runs out he puts his egg into a pan of boiling water, removing it when the five-minute timer runs out.

## 20
### FAMOUS SHIPS

Endeavour = Captain Cook
Golden Hind = Francis Drake
Mayflower = Pilgrim Fathers
Santa Maria = Christopher Columbus
Victory = Lord Nelson.

## 21
### IT'S ALL RELATIVE

My son.

## 22
### WHICH IS GREATER?

Six dozen dozen (864) is greater than half a dozen dozen (72).

## 23
### COUNTRY NAMES

(a) DAN
(b) ADA
(c) PHILIP
(d) ERICA
(e) DON
(f) TINA
(g) ALAN
(h) ALI
(i) RITA
(j) GARY.

## 24
### TWO COINS

A 50 pence piece and a 5 pence piece. One of the coins is not a 50 pence piece, but the other is!

## 25
### SPOTTY DOGS

One spotty dog has thirty-nine spots, and the other has fifty-seven spots.

## 26
### FIVE-LETTER BIRDS

RAVEN.

## 27
### DON AND CARL

When they pass they are obviously both the same distance from Doncaster!

## 28
### A FIRST-CLASS PUZZLE

Half of them.

## 29
### SANDWICH FILLING

MARMALADE.

## 30
### CONSECUTIVE ODD NUMBERS

9, 11, 13.

## 31
### MISSING GIRLS

(a) ANN
(b) EVE
(c) SUE
(d) LIZ
(e) AMY
(f) PAM
(g) EVA
(h) ADA.

## 32
### SAVINGS

Thirty-two 5p coins and twelve 20p coins.

## 33
### SPELLING TEST

The following words are incorrect: PARALEL (should be PARALLEL), WIERDNESS (should be WEIRDNESS), SEPERATE (should be SEPARATE) and COMITTEE (should be COMMITTEE).

## 34
### GRANDFATHER AND GRANDSON

Their ages are 60 and 16.

## 35
### LITTER CHANCE

(a) Old Father Time
(b) Get rich quick
(c) Might and main
(d) Jolly good fellow
(e) Money for jam
(f) Last but not least
(g) Dance for joy
(h) Wild goose chase.

## 36
### WHAT'S THE SPORT?

Tug-of-war.

## 37
### A PIECE OF CAKE

36 ounces (1021 grammes), or 2¼ lb (1.02 kilogrammes).

## 38
## BOOMERANG BALL

Throw it straight up in the air!

## 39
## A TALE OF FOUR CITIES

Deltaville.

## 40
## FIVE-LETTER COUNTRIES

LIBYA.

## 41
## RACING RESULTS

First was Clare, followed by Alison, Bunty, Debby and finally Emma.

## 42
## FRUIT

A melon costs 62p, a coconut 57p and a pineapple 83p.

## 43
## WORK IT OUT

44.

## 44
## MISSING BOYS

| | | | |
|---|---|---|---|
| (a) | LEO | (e) | SID |
| (b) | TOM | (f) | ALF |
| (c) | ROY | (g) | IAN |
| (d) | KEN | (h) | ALI. |

## 45
## BUYING SWEETS

She started with £4.95 and spent £1.95.

## 46
## WHAT'S MY LINE?

| | | | |
|---|---|---|---|
| (a) | BAKER | (f) | SURVEYOR |
| (b) | BUTCHER | (g) | POSTMAN |
| (c) | TEACHER | (h) | POLICEMAN |
| (d) | CHEMIST | (i) | SECRETARY |
| (e) | SURGEON | (j) | ELECTRICIAN. |

## 47
## FIVE-LETTER CAPITALS

CAIRO.

## 48
## ROUND THE CLOCK

Ten times.

## 49
## AIRLINES

| | | | |
|---|---|---|---|
| (a) | Ireland | (e) | Israel |
| (b) | Netherlands | (f) | USSR |
| (c) | Australia | (g) | West Germany |
| (d) | USA | (h) | Belgium. |

## 50
## NOUGHTS AND CROSSES

Every game should be drawn. If the first player takes the centre, the second should take a corner or lose. If the first player takes a corner, the second must take the centre or lose. If the first player starts with a side, both must play carefully. But every game should be drawn, unless one player blunders.

## 51
## FILM STARS

| | | | |
|---|---|---|---|
| (a) | John Wayne | (g) | Glenda Jackson |
| (b) | Humphrey Bogart | (h) | Paul Newman |
| (c) | Julie Andrews | (i) | Hayley Mills |
| (d) | Sylvester Stallone | (j) | Marlon Brando |
| (e) | Barbra Streisand | (k) | Robert Mitchum |
| (f) | Steve McQueen | (l) | Goldie Hawn. |

## 52
## FIND THE NUMBER

126.

## 53
## SPORTING PLACES

(a) Tennis
(b) Cricket
(c) Golf
(d) Horse-racing
(e) Rugby Union
(f) Motor-cycle racing
(g) Yachting
(h) Rifle-shooting.

### 54
### COMPLETE THE COUNTRIES

| | | | |
|---|---|---|---|
| (a) | AUSTRIA | (d) | MOROCCO |
| (b) | ALGERIA | (e) | ALBANIA |
| (c) | LIBERIA | (f) | LEBANON. |

### 55
### TOM, DICK AND HARRY

Tom receives $210, Dick $191 and Harry $174.

### 56
### DIGGORY'S HOLE

4 feet (1.2 metres).

### 57
### LEFT-HANDED TEAPOTS

15.

### 58
### ON THE STREET WHERE I LIVE

116.

### 59
### A BRIDGE PROBLEM

840 feet (256 metres).

### 60
### POTATOES

1056, 1232 and 1386.

### 61
### EUSTACE AND HILDA

Hilda is 28.

### 62
### A TRIP TO THE SEASIDE

He sold twenty-two tickets.

### 63
### BOOK CHOICE

I could choose an arithmetic book and a geometry book in 8 × 10 or 80 ways. I could choose an arithmetic book and an algebra book in 8 × 12 or 96 ways. I could choose a geometry book and an algebra book in 10 × 12 or 120 ways.

There is therefore a total of 296 different ways in which I could choose two books.

### 64
### JACK AND JILL

2¼ miles (3.6 kilometres).

### 65
### ON THE BUSES

Mr Bus is fifty-four and Mrs Bus is forty-five.

### 66
### A FOWL QUESTION

Twenty-four.

### 67
### MULTIPLES OF SEVEN

259, 266, 273, 280, 287, 294 and 301.

### 68
### YOUNG ROTHSCHILD

He had seven 50p coins, ten 20p coins and thirty 5p coins.

### 69
### THE WIDOW'S LEGACY

$7500.

### 70
### LONGFELLOW'S BEES

Fifteen.

### 71
### WINE AND WATER

The wine in the small glass was one-sixth of the total liquid and the wine in the large glass was two-ninths of the total. Add these together and we find that the wine was seven-eighteenths of the total, and therefore the water was eleven-eighteenths.

### 72
### CRICKET SCORES

The scores were as follows: Archer 56, Baxter 48, Clifford 24 and Dexter 16.

### 73
### SHARE DEALING

£2250.

## 74
## UPSTREAM, DOWNSTREAM

300 miles (483 kilometres).

## 75
## REMAINDERS

The number is 2519.

## 76
## MILES AND MINUTES

$x$ must be the square root of 60, approximately 7.745.

## 77
## THE UNIVERSAL FRIENDLY SOCIETY

At the first meeting there were 105 handshakes. At the second meeting there were 21 members present. For $n$ members, the number of handshakes is given by the formula

$$\frac{n(n-1)}{2}$$

## 78
## VATRIQUANT'S CRYPTARITHM

```
  125
   37 ×

  875
  375

 4625
```

In the second partial product, we see D × A = D, hence A = 1. D × C and E × C both end in C, hence C = 5. D and E must be odd. Since both partial products have only three digits, neither can be 9. This leaves only 3 and 7. In the first partial product, E × B is a number of two digits, while in the second partial product, D × B is a number of only one digit. Thus E is larger than D, so E = 7 and D = 3.

Since D × B has only one digit, B must be 3 or less. The only two possibilities are 0 and 2. B cannot be 0 because 7B is a two digit number. Thus B = 2. By completing the multiplication, F = 8, G = 6, H = 4.

## 79
## SEND MORE MONEY

```
  9567
  1085 +

 10652
```

## 80
## TWO × TWO = THREE

$138 \times 138 = 19044$

Since THREE contains five digits, T must equal 1 and W less than or equal to 4. E = 4 because 44 is the only combination of two equal digits that can terminate a square (except for 00, which does not apply here). Hence O = 2 or 8. TWO must therefore be 128, 138 or 132, and a quick trial shows that 138 is the only possibility.

## 81
## I MEND DENIM

$8 \times 4973 = 39784$

## 82
## A PRESIDENTIAL PUZZLE

```
 570140
      6 ×

3420840
```

## 83
## A NEW DEAL PUZZLE

$178 + 230 = 408$

$178 + 408 = 586$

## 84
## FLY FOR YOUR LIFE

```
  598
  507
 8047 +

 9152
```

## 85
### SCRABBLE

```
  7088062
17531908 +
─────────
24619970
═════════
```

## 86
### THE SOLITARY SEVEN

```
        97809
124)12128316
    1116
    ────
     968
     868
    ────
    1003
     992
    ────
     1116
     1116
```

## 87
### THE SIX NOUGHTS

```
 100
 330
 505
 077
 099
────
1111
```

## 88
### GRANT'S SON AND GRANDSON

Let a = Grant's age, b = his son's age, and c = his grandson's age. From the information given, we can produce these equations:

$$a + b = 100$$
$$a = 5c$$
$$c + (a - b) = b + 8$$

From these equations we can derive the fact that a = 65, hence b = 35 and c = 13. So Grant's grandson is 13.

## 89
### THE RAJAH'S DIAMONDS

There must have been six sons and thirty-six diamonds. Working backwards, it is obvious that the last son must have received the seventh part of nothing, or there would have been some diamonds remaining. It is also clear that there must be a difference of six between the numbers dealt with at successive operations. The rest is then easy.

## 90
### ROOTS

The easiest way of solving this problem is to raise both numbers to the power of 13, giving $10^3$ (= 1000) and $2^{10}$ (= 1024).

Obviously, then, the cube root of 2 is larger.

## 91
### FAIR SHARES

The man who produced five loaves should receive seven cents, and the one who brought three loaves should receive one cent.

## 92
### REGISTRATIONS

The theoretical maximum is 17,558,424 (999 × 26 × 26 × 26). This number is reduced by 999 for every embarrassing three-letter combination.

## 93
### SHARING A BICYCLE

Let Sturmey ride 11⅑ miles (17.7 kilometres), drop the bicycle, and walk the rest of the way. Archer will walk until he picks up the bicycle and then ride to their destination, getting there at the same time as Sturmey. The journey takes them three hours twenty minutes.

## 94
### DIVIDING THE CORN

The landlord would lose 7⅕ sackfuls by the proposed arrangement. Suppose there were only 100 sackfuls in all (any figures will do), then the tenant was entitled to 60 and the landlord to 40. But, as proposed, the tenant would get 67⅓ and the landlord only 32⅘.

The tenant should give the landlord 18 sackfuls from his own share after the division of the remainder is completed. This will be found to work out all right.

## 95
## THE WEIGHING-MACHINE FRAUD

Call the children A, B, C, D, E in order of their weights, A being the lightest and E the heaviest. It is clear that A and B (the lightest) together weigh 114 lb (51.7 kg), and D and E (the heaviest) 129 lb (58.5 kg), so these four together weigh 243 lb (110 kg) – which, deducted from the weight of all five, 303 lb (137 kg), gives us the weight of C – 60 lb (27 kg). (To obtain the 303 lb (137 kg), add all the pairs together and divide by 4, since each child was weighed four times.)

The lightest and next lightest but one weighed 115 lb (52 kg) – that is A and C – so the weight of A must be 55 lb (25 kg). The rest is now quite easy, and the children weighed respectively 55 lb (25 kg), 59 lb (26.8 kg), 60 lb (27 kg), 63 lb (28.6 kg) and 66 lb (30 kg).

## 96
## NON-PRIMES

The integers from 1001! + 2 to 1001! + 1001 are all non-prime. (1001! + 2 is divisible by 2, 1001! + 3 by 3, and so on to 1001! + 1001 which is divisible by 1001.)

## 97
## BETELGEUSIAN MATHEMATICS

The number system we are most commonly acquainted with is decimal (i.e. base 10). In this system 1552 means $(1 \times 10^3) + (5 \times 10^2) + (5 \times 10) + 2$.

We sometimes use other number bases, for example in computer software we may use binary (base 2), octal (base 8) or hexadecimal (base 16).

Betelgeusian mathematics uses the septal system (base 7). Here 1552 means $(1 \times 7^3) + (5 \times 7^2) + (5 \times 7) + 2$, which is equivalent to 625 (decimal). Hence the answer is 34 (Betelgeusian) which is equivalent to 25 (decimal).

## 98
## PRIME FACTORS

There are nineteen such numbers:

| | |
|---|---|
| 30 = 2.3.5 | 110 = 2.5.11 |
| 42 = 2.3.7. | 130 = 2.5.13 |
| 66 = 2.3.11 | 170 = 2.5.17 |
| 78 = 2.3.13 | 190 = 2.5.19 |
| 102 = 2.3.17 | 154 = 2.7.11 |
| 114 = 2.3.19 | 182 = 2.7.13 |
| 138 = 2.3.23 | 105 = 3.5.7 |
| 174 = 2.3.29 | 165 = 3.5.11 |
| 186 = 2.3.31 | 195 = 3.5.13 |
| 70 = 2.5.7 | |

## 99
## CONFUSING DATES

The days that are ambiguous are the first twelve days of each month, excluding January 1st, February 2nd, March 3rd, etc. That is, eleven days each month. The number of ambiguous days is therefore 132, giving a percentage of approximately 36.16 (36.07% in a leap year).

## 100
## THE NEW STUDENTS

The number of new students was 1416 (which is the sum of 157, 472 and 787 – the only three numbers meeting the given conditions).

## 101
## THE SOOPER MICROCOMPUTER

We need to factorize 223,427 and 363,593. Each of these numbers is the product of two primes:

$$223,427 = 373 \times 599$$
$$363,593 = 607 \times 599$$

The price must therefore be $599.

## 102
## ROOT EXTRACTION

The only other numbers are 5832, 17576 and 19683, the cube roots of which may be correctly obtained by merely adding the digits which come to 18, 26 and 27 respectively.

## 103
## 111111

The sum of the divisors is 204288.

There is a remarkable formula for calculating the sum of the divisors of a number, which avoids the necessity of enumerating all the divisors. First, we have to express the number as a product of its prime factors – in this case $111,111 = 3 \times 7 \times 11 \times 13 \times 37$. Since no prime factor is repeated, all we have to do is add one to each of the prime factors and form a product. So the sum of the divisors of $111,111 = 4 \times 8 \times 12 \times 14 \times 38 = 204288$.

## 104
## NO REPEATS

The answer is 8,887,690.

Since we can't admit integers beginning with zero, there are 9 possibilities (1 to 9) for the leading digit position, and 10 possibilities (0 to 9) for the other positions. The easiest way of tackling the problem is to find the number of integers complying with the condition, according to the number of digits in the integer.

1-digit integers = 9
2-digit integers = $9 \times 9$
3-digit integers = $9 \times 9 \times 8$
4-digit integers = $9 \times 9 \times 8 \times 7$
5-digit integers = $9 \times 9 \times 8 \times 7 \times 6$
6-digit integers = $9 \times 9 \times 8 \times 7 \times 6 \times 5$
7-digit integers = $9 \times 9 \times 8 \times 7 \times 6 \times 5 \times 4$
8-digit integers = $9 \times 9 \times 8 \times 7 \times 6 \times 5 \times 4 \times 3$
9-digit integers = $9 \times 9 \times 8 \times 7 \times 6 \times 5 \times 4 \times 3 \times 2$
10-digit integers = $9 \times 9 \times 8 \times 7 \times 6 \times 5 \times 4 \times 3 \times 2 \times 1$

(Obviously, no integer of more than 10 digits will qualify.)

## 105
## DIGITAL MULTIPLICATION

There are nine solutions:

| | |
|---|---|
| $5796 = 483 \times 12$ | $7632 = 159 \times 48$ |
| $5796 = 138 \times 42$ | $4396 = 157 \times 28$ |
| $5346 = 297 \times 18$ | $6952 = 1738 \times 4$ |
| $5346 = 198 \times 27$ | $7852 = 1963 \times 4$ |
| $7254 = 186 \times 39$ | |

## 106
## CATS AND MICE

There were 239 cats and each cat killed 4649 mice.

## 107
## TELEPHONE NUMBERS

My number is 665857. The Professor's is 470832.

(The square of 665857 is 443,365,544,449 and the square of 470832 is 221,682,772,224.)

## 108
## TWO-STROKE GOLF

The course can be completed in twenty-six shots by using a 150-yard (137-metre) drive and a 125-yard (114-metre) approach. The shots are made as follows:

150 yards (137 metres): 1 drive
300 yards (274 metres): 2 drives
250 yards (229 metres): 2 approaches
325 yards (297 metres): 3 drives, 1 approach back
275 yards (251 metres): 1 drive, 1 approach
350 yards (320 metres): 4 approaches, 1 drive back
225 yards (206 metres): 3 approaches, 1 drive back
400 yards (366 metres): 1 drive, 2 approaches
425 yards (389 metres): 2 drives, 1 approach

## 109
## THE CAT AND DOG RACE

The cat wins, of course. It has to make precisely 100 leaps to complete the distance and return. The dog, on the contrary, is compelled to go 102 feet (31.1 metres) and back. Its thirty-third leap takes it to the 99-foot (30-metre) mark and so another leap, carrying it 2 feet (⅔ metre) beyond the mark, becomes necessary. In all, the dog must make 68 leaps to go the distance. But it jumps only two-thirds as quickly as the cat, so that while the cat is making 100 leaps the dog cannot make quite 67.

But Barnum had an April Fool possibility up his sleeve. Suppose that the cat is male and the dog is female! The phrase 'she makes three leaps to his two' would then mean that the dog would go 9 feet (2.7 metres) while the cat went 4 (1.2). Thus when the dog finishes the race in 68 leaps, the cat will have travelled only 90 feet 8 inches (27.2 metres).

## 110
### THE MISER'S PUZZLE

Because the miser could divide each type of coin evenly into four, five and six parts, he must have had not less than sixty coins of each type, making a total of $2100.

## 111
### CARNIVAL DICE GAME

Out of the 216 equally probable ways the dice may be thrown, you will win on only 91 of them, lose on 125. So your chance of winning at least as much as you bet is 91/216, your chance of losing 125/216.

If the dice always showed different numbers, the game would be a fair one. Suppose all the squares were covered with a dollar. The operator would on each roll that showed three different numbers, take in three dollars and pay out three. But on doubles he makes a dollar and on triples he makes two dollars. In the long run, for every dollar wagered by a player, regardless of how he places the money and in what amounts, he can expect to lose about 7.8 cents. This gives the operator a profit of 7.8 per cent on each dollar bet.

## 112
### THE ANNUAL PICNIC

900 picnickers started for the picnic in 100 wagons, 9 to a wagon.

## 113
### OLD BEACON TOWER

If you draw one of the diagonals on a rectangular sheet of paper, then roll the sheet into a cylinder, the diagonal will form a spiral around the cylinder. In other words, a spiral around a column may be regarded as the hypotenuse of a right triangle. In this case, it is a right triangle wrapped four times around the column. The base of this triangle is four times the circumference of the cylinder (*pi* times the diameter times four), which proves to be a negligible fraction above 300 feet (91.5 metres). This is also the height of the tower, which is just a coincidence because the height does not enter at all into the solution of the problem.

Nor do we have to consider the length of the stairway. For if pickets are a foot apart on the base of a right triangle, the same number will be the same distance apart on the hypotenuse regardless of how long it is. Since the base of our right triangle is 300 feet (91.5 metres), there would be 300 steps on the circular stairs.

## 114
### THE ECCENTRIC TEACHER

The first girl was just 638 days old, and the boy twice as much, namely 1276 days. The next day the youngest girl will be 639 days old, and her new recruit 1915 days, totalling 2554 days which doubles that of the first boy who, having gained one day, will be 1277 days old. The next day the boy, being 1278 days old, brings his big brother, who is 3834 days old, so their combined ages amount to 5112 days, just twice the combined ages of the girls who will now be 640 and 1916, totalling 2556.

The next day, the girls gaining one day each, will represent 2558 days, which added to 7670 days of the last recruit, brings their sum total to 10 228 days, just twice that of the two boys, which would now be increased to 5114 days.

Those who gave the boy's age as 3½ years overlooked the feature of increasing the ages of the pupils from day to day.

## 115
## FALSE WEIGHTS

If the broker weighed the goods with a pound (450 gramme) weight 1 ounce (28 grammes) too heavy, he got 17 ounces (481 grammes) for a pound (450 grammes). When he sold them by a weight 1 ounce (28 grammes) light he gave 15 ounces (425 grammes) for a pound (450 grammes), and had 2 ounces (56 grammes) over. If these 2 ounces (56 grammes) were sold at the same price, so as to make $25 by cheating, it is plain that the 2 ounces (56 grammes) represent $\frac{2}{15}$ of what he paid for the whole and charged for the 15 ounces (425 grammes). One-fifteenth being worth $12.50, fifteen-fifteenths, or the whole, would be $187.50, which, if there was no question of commission, would be what he paid for the goods.

We find, however, that he received 2 per cent from the seller, $3.75, and $4.25 from the purchaser, making $8 brokerage in addition to $25 by cheating. Now, if he had dealt honestly, he would have paid for 17 ounces (28 grammes), which, to be exact, would have been $199.21875. His brokerage for buying and selling would therefore only be $7.96875, so he has made an additional $3\frac{1}{8}$ cents by cheating. As the story said that he made exactly $25 by cheating, we must reduce the $187.50 price so that his two cheatings will amount to just $25.

Now, as 3 and $\frac{1}{8}$ cents is exactly $\frac{1}{801}$ part of $25.03125, we must reduce $187.50 by its $\frac{1}{801}$ part, which will bring it down to $187.27, so that he will make just $25 and .0006 of a cent by cheating. To such as wish to be very exact, I would suggest that the seller be paid $187.2659176029973125 less the 2 per cent brokerage of $3.745 plus.

## 116
## WEIGHING THE TEA

(1)  With the 5 lb and 9 lb weights in different pans weigh 4 lb.
(2)  With the 4 lb weigh second 4 lb.
(3)  Weigh third 4 lb.
(4)  Weigh fourth 4 lb, and the remainder will be 4 lb.
(5), (6), (7), (8), (9)  Divide each portion of 4 lb in turn equally on the two sides of the scales.

## 117
## A COMMON DIVISOR

Since the numbers have a common factor plus the same remainder, if the numbers are subtracted from one another in the manner shown below the results must contain the common factor without the remainder.

$$508\,811 \atop 480\,608\ - \over 28\,203 \qquad 723\,217 \atop 508\,811\ - \over 214\,406$$

The prime factors of 28 203 are 3, 7, 17, 79, and those of 214, 406 are 2, 23, 59, 79. Therefore the required divisor is 79, the only factor common to both, and the common remainder will be found to be 51. Simple, is it not?

## 118
## COW, GOAT AND GOOSE

As cow and goat eat $\frac{1}{45}$ in a day, cow and goose $\frac{1}{60}$ in a day, and goat and goose $\frac{1}{90}$ in a day, we soon find that the cow eats $\frac{5}{360}$ in a day, the goat $\frac{3}{360}$ in a day, and the goose $\frac{1}{360}$ in a day. Therefore, together they will eat $\frac{9}{360}$ in a day, or $\frac{1}{40}$. So they will eat all the grass in the field in 40 days, since there is no growth of grass in the meantime.

## 119
## A FAIR DISTRIBUTION

The number of children must be even, and either two, six, or fourteen. But there was an equal number of 'boys and girls', and one boy and one girl are not 'boys and girls'. Therefore two is excluded. In the case of fourteen, each child must receive one halfpenny orange only; but one orange is not 'oranges'. We are, therefore, driven back on our third case, which exactly fulfils the conditions. Three boys and three girls each receive one halfpenny orange and two three-a-penny oranges, the value of which is together one penny and one-sixth, or one sixth of sevenpence.

## 120
## THE SEE-SAW PUZZLE

The boy's weight must have been about 39.79 lb (18.04 kg). A brick weighed 3 lb (1.36 kg). Therefore sixteen bricks weighed 48 lb (21.77 kg) and eleven bricks 33 lb (14.96 kg). Multiply 48 by 33 and take the square root.

## 121
## THE DISPATCH RIDER

The answer is the square root of twice the square of 40, added to 40. This is 96.568 miles.

## 122
## THE TOWER OF PISA

The ball would come to rest after travelling 218 ft 9⅓ in (800.2 metres).

## 123
## HOW OLD WAS MARY?

The age of Mary to that of Ann must be as 5 to 3. And as the sum of their ages was 44, Mary was 27½ and Ann 16½. One is exactly 11 years older than the other.

I will now insert in brackets in the original statement the various ages specified: 'Mary is (27½) twice as old as Ann was (13¾) when Mary was half as old (24¾) as Ann will be (49½) when Ann is three times as old (49½) as Mary was (16½) when Mary was (16½) three times as old as Ann (5½).'

Now check this backwards. When Mary was three times as old as Ann, Mary was 16½ and Ann 5½ (11 years younger). Then we get 49½ for the age Ann will be when she is three times as old as Mary was then. When Mary was half this she was 24¾. And at that time Ann must have been 13¾ (11 years younger). Therefore Mary is now twice as old – 27½, and Ann 11 years younger – 16½.

## 124
## MONKEY AND PULLEY

We find the age of the monkey works out at 1½ years, and the age of the mother 2½ years, the monkey therefore weighing 2½ lb (1.1 kilogrammes), and the weight the same. Then we soon discover that the rope weighed 1¼ lb (0.6 kilogramme), or 20 oz (567 grammes); and, as a foot weighed 4 oz (113 grammes), the length of the rope was 5 ft (1.5 metres).

## 125
## THE TRAVELLERS

Spurs.

## 126
## OLD MOTHER TWITCHETT

A needle and thread.

## 127
## THE BEGINNING OF ETERNITY

The letter E.

## 129
## THE RIVAL BROTHERS

A pair of dice.

## 130
## TWO LEGS SAT UPON THREE LEGS

That is a woman with two legs sat on a stool with three legs, and had a leg of mutton in her hand; then came a dog that hath four legs, and bare away the leg of mutton; then up start the woman, and threw the stool with three legs at the dog with four legs, and brought again the leg of mutton.

## 131
## HE WENT TO THE WOOD

That is a thorn; for a man went to the wood, and caught a thorn in his foot, and then he sat him down, and sought to have pulled it out, and because he could not find it out, he must needs bring it home.

## 132
## AN ENIGMA BY JONATHAN SWIFT

A lady's fan.

## 133
## AN ENIGMA BY HORACE WALPOLE

Today.

## 134
## AN ENIGMA BY VOLTAIRE

Time.

## 135
## 'TWAS WHISPERED IN HEAVEN

The letter H.

## 136
## CAN YOU TELL ME WHY?

The eye of deceit
Can best counterfeit
And so, I suppose,
Can best count 'er toes.

## 137
### ALPHABETICAL CONUNDRUMS

The answers are as follows:

A – because it is the middle of DAY.
B – because it makes OIL BOIL.
C – because it makes CLASSES of LASSES.
D – because it is an extremity of LAND.
E – because it is the end of LIFE.
F – because it is the capital of FRANCE.
G – because it makes a LAD GLAD.
H – because it makes the EAR HEAR.
I – because it is the centre of BLISS.
J – because it is close to the eye (I).
K – because it is the end of PORK.
L – because it makes OVER a LOVER.
M – because it makes ORE MORE.
N – because it makes A STY NASTY.
O – because all the others are in AUDIBLE (inaudible).
P – because it makes A PA.
Q – because it is always followed by you (U).
R – because it is next to Kew (Q).
S – because it makes HOT SHOT.
T – because it is in the middle of WATER.
U – because it is always in TROUBLE and DIFFICULTIES.
V – because it is always in LOVE.
W – because it makes ILL WILL.
X – because it stands for annex (an X).
Y – because it is in the middle of the EYE.
Z – because it is to be found in the ZOO.

## 138
### HISTORY MYSTERIES

1 Adam – he was first in the human race.
2 They turned on the Israelites.
3 Samson – he brought the house down.
4 Because God told them to multiply on the face of the earth.
5 To get to the other side.
6 The Anglo-Saxophone.
7 Because there were so many knights.
8 Old King Cole.
9 Because he liked to chop and change.
10 At the bottom.
11 Before U and I were born.
12 Florence of Arabia.

## 139
### CAREER CONUNDRUMS

1 They fight tooth and nail.
2 He throws them overboard and they get washed ashore.
3 Because he has lots to sell.
4 Because they have lots of dough but are always kneading more.
5 When they are down in the dumps.
6 Because his career was in ruins.
7 Because they know their tables.
8 Because they are both face workers.
9 Law suits.
10 Because their job makes them sell fish.
11 The Burrow Surveyor.
12 When they provide a service.

## 140
### ANIMAL CRACKERS

1 A zebra with measles.
2 Iceburgers.
3 A wild bore.
4 Croaka-cola.
5 Moths – they only eat holes.
6 Because they would look silly in macintoshes.
7 Because their horns don't work.
8 Because it crew so.
9 Because it's too far to walk.
10 Because it's a huge undertaking.
11 Because its head is so far from its body.
12 Drop it a line.

## 141
### WHAT'S THE DIFFERENCE?

1  One roars with pain, the other pours with rain.
2  One mends a tear, the other tends a mare.
3  One is hard up, the other is soft down.
4  One hits his missus, the other misses his hits.
5  One is a female, the other is a mail fee.
6  One steals from the people, the other peels from the steeple.
7  An elephant can have fleas, but a flea can't have elephants.
8  One knows his blows, the other blows his nose.
9  One baits his hooks, the other hates his books.
10 One watches birds, the other botches words.
11 One makes acorns, the other makes corns ache.
12 One gets tanned by the sun, the other gets sand by the ton.

## 142
### SUGAR LUMPS

Place two lumps in the first cup, one lump in the second, and seven lumps in the third. If you place the second cup in the first cup, there will then be a total of three in the first cup.

## 143
### SALT

Rub a nylon comb on your sleeve, then hold it above the salt. Static electricity will do the rest.

## 144
### TYING THE KNOT

Fold your arms before picking up the ends of the string. Then, when you unfold your arms the string will have a knot in it.

## 145
### CATCH 'EM

Having thrown and caught the first lump, simply let go of the second and catch it by lowering the glass quickly.

## 146
### A FUNNEL PUZZLE

The obvious way is to put the narrow end of the funnel to your mouth and blow through it. But you will never blow the candle out that way. What you have to do is blow through the broad end of the funnel, pointing the narrow end at the candle.

## 147
### LIFT THE ICE-CUBE

Fold the piece of string in half and lower the centre portion until it is resting on the ice-cube. Now sprinkle some salt over the string and ice-cube, and wait a few seconds. The salt will make some of the ice melt and re-freeze over the string. Now lift both ends of the string and up comes the ice-cube!

## 148
### THE BOTTLED EGG

The egg is soaked in vinegar until the shell becomes so soft that the egg can simply be pushed through the neck of the bottle. The bottle is then rinsed out with cold water to remove the smell of vinegar and to make the eggshell hard again.

## 149
### FLOAT THE CORK

The secret is simply that the glass of water must be absolutely full to the brim. The cork will then float quite happily in the centre.

## 150
### SNAP!

Place the matchstick so that it lies along the end of your forefinger, and hold it in place with your thumb. Now simply bend your forefinger, while pressing with your thumb, and the match will snap.

## 151
### KEEP IT DRY

Cram the handkerchief well down into the glass, and hold the tumbler upside down. If you plunge the glass straight down into the water, an air bubble will be trapped at the top of the glass and this ensures that the handkerchief stays dry.

## 152
### AN OVERBLOWN PUZZLE

Gently blow the card towards the edge of the table until part of it is projecting over the edge. Then kneel down and give the card a short sharp blow from beneath. The card will then turn over.

## 153
### A FINANCIAL BALANCE

It can be done, though it needs a steady hand. First bend the folded note so that it forms a right-angle, then balance the coin at the centre of the fold. Now carefully straighten out the bend and, with luck, the coin will remain balanced on the top.

## 154
### CUT!

When you tie the string to the door handle you use a bow knot. Then, you can simply cut one of the loops of the bow – you will have cut the string and of course the cup remains suspended.

## 155
### THE ODD KING

The King of Hearts.

## 156
### A TRICK WITH DICE

All you have to do is subtract 250 from the result given, and the three figures in the answer will represent the values of the three dice. Thus, a result of 875 would mean the values of the dice are 6, 2 and 5.

## 157
### CUNNING COINS

| | | | |
|---|---|---|---|
| (a) | Temple | (e) | Lid |
| (b) | Neck | (f) | Lash |
| (c) | Brow | (g) | Two lips (Tulips). |
| (d) | Eye (I) | | |

## 158
### HEADS AND TAILS

Move coins 1 and 2 to the right of coin 6. Move coins 6 and 1 to the right of coin 2. Move coins 3 and 4 to the right of coin 5.

## 159
### BLOW!

The secret is to blow, not at the coin, but into the mouth of the glass. The outer edge of the card will tilt, and the coin will slide into the glass.

## 160
### COIN CROSS

Take the bottom two coins from the vertical arm and stack them on top of the centre coin, making five coins in both directions.

## 161
### THE PAPER BAND PUZZLE

Give one end of the strip just half a turn before joining the ends, so that the loop has a slight twist in it. Now, when you draw your line, the paper will seem to have one side only. Try it and see!

## 162
### FOUR IN A ROW

Place nine coins in a square array to form three rows of three. Now place another coin on top of the first coin in the first row, another on top of the second coin in the second row, and another on top of the third coin in the third row.

You now have three horizontal rows and three vertical rows, and each row contains four coins.

## 163
### TURNOVER

Hold the cover in your hand, place your mouth over the end of the cover, and suck as hard as you can. This produces a partial vacuum, making the tray stick to the cover. Now tilt your head back so that the tray is on top, and carefully place the cover back on the table.

## 164
### THREE AND A HALF DOZEN

Lay down three of the matches – one, two, three. Now lay down the other three matches so as to form the Roman numerals VI. Now you have made 'three and a half dozen'.

## 165
## MATCHEMATICS

Use the eight matches to form the Roman numerals XII (four matches for the X, two for each I). Now remove half the matches – the lower four – and you will be left with the Roman numerals VII, thus proving that half of twelve is seven.

## 166
## MORE MATCHEMATICS

Arrange the matches to spell the word FIVE, using three matches for F, one for I, two for V, and four for E. If you take away the F and E (seven of the ten matches) you will be left with IV, the Roman numerals for 4.

## 167
## A PUSH-OVER

If you are female, you will almost certainly be able to do this. If you are male you will almost certainly fail. The ability to perform this feat seems to be related to the shape of the pelvis, which is different in men and women.

## 168
## HOW MANY LEFT?

The result will always be four greater than the original difference.

## 169
## A CIRCLE OF COINS

Skip over one coin each time before starting on the next count.

## 170
## A COIN TRICK

The pile of six coins should be in the following order, reading the upper faces from top to bottom: head, tail, tail, tail, head, head. The trick is even more perplexing if you assume an indifference to the number of coins and sometimes use five (arranged head, head, tail, tail, head) or seven coins (arranged head, tail, tail, head, head, tail, tail).

## 171
## ORANGES AND APPLES

Number the plates in order round the circle and place the oranges and apples alternately on plates 1–10 leaving 11 and 12 blank. Then remove from 2 and 3, 7 and 8, 4 and 5, 10 and 11, and 1 and 2 (or 8 and 9). All the apples will then be together, all the oranges together, and two adjacent plates empty.

## 172
## DOMINO 23

Use these four dominoes in this order: 1:1, 4:4, 4:3 and 3:3.

## 173
## THE TEN CARDS

The first player can always win. He should first turn down the third card from one of the ends, leaving them thus: 00 × 0000000. Now, whatever the second player does, the first can always leave either 000 × 000 or 0 × 00 × 000.

In the first case, whatever the second player does in one group of three, the other repeats in the other group of three, until he gets the last card.

In the second case, whatever the second player does, the first can always leave either 0 × 0 or 0 × 0 × 0 × 0 or 00 × 00, and gets an obvious win.

## 174
## ROOK AND BISHOP

Suppose the rook is placed on one of the 4 centre squares. It threatens 14 squares and is threatened diagonally from 13 squares. This gives a total of 27 threatened/threatening squares out of 63.

Similarly, we get a total of 25 for each of the twelve squares bordering the centre, 23 for each of the squares bordering these, and 21 for each square of the outer border.

The probability is therefore:

$$\frac{4}{64} \times \frac{27}{63} + \frac{12}{64} \times \frac{25}{63} + \frac{20}{64} \times \frac{23}{63} + \frac{28}{64} \times \frac{21}{63} = \frac{13}{16}$$

## 175
## CHESS ROUTES

The total number of different routes is 48,639. This answer is arrived at as follows. In an 8 by 8 grid write the number of ways there are of reaching each square from the top left-hand square. Here is the start of such a grid:

| 1 | 1 | 1 | 1 | 1 | 1 | 1 | 1 |
|---|---|---|---|---|---|---|---|
| 1 | 3 | 5 | 7 | 9 | 11 | 13 | 15 |
| 1 | 5 | 13 | 25 | 41 | 61 | 85 | |
| 1 | 7 | 25 | 63 | | | | |
| 1 | 9 | 41 | | | | | |
| 1 | 11 | 61 | | | | | |
| 1 | 13 | 85 | | | | | |
| 1 | 15 | | | | | | |

The number for each square may be found by adding the number to the left of it, the number diagonally to the left and up, and the number above it.

## 176
## THE TRAVELLING ROOK

The minimum number of moves is sixteen.

## 177
## THE PEBBLE GAME

In the case of fifteen pebbles, the first player wins if he first takes two. Then when he holds an odd number and leaves one, eight or nine in the pile he wins, and when he holds an even number and leaves four, five or twelve he also wins. He can always do one or other of these things until the end of the game, and so defeat his opponent.

In the case of thirteen pebbles the first player must lose if his opponent plays correctly. In fact, the only numbers with which the first player ought to lose are five and multiples of eight added to five, such as thirteen, twenty-one, twenty-nine, etc.

## 178
## SOLITAIRE

Here is one of the many solutions. Referring to the numbers on the diagram, make the following moves: 19 to 17, 16 to 18, 29 to 17, 17 to 19, 30 to 18, 27 to 25, 22 to 24, 24 to 26, 31 to 23, 4 to 16, 16 to 28, 7 to 9, 10 to 8, 12 to 10, 3 to 11, 18 to 6, 1 to 3, 3 to 11, 13 to 27, 27 to 25, 21 to 7, 7 to 9, 33 to 31, 31 to 23, 10 to 8, 8 to 22, 22 to 24, 24 to 26, 26 to 12, 12 to 10, 5 to 17.

## 179
## UPSIDE DOWN

NOON.

## 180
## CLICHES

| | | | |
|---|---|---|---|
| (a) | Gild the lily | (f) | Spill the beans |
| (b) | Bury the hatchet | (g) | Kick the bucket |
| (c) | Run the gauntlet | (h) | Beard the lion |
| (d) | Beat about the bush | (i) | Turn the tables |
| (e) | Face the music | (j) | Toe the line. |

## 181
## IN WHOLE AND IN PART

| | | | |
|---|---|---|---|
| (1) | Tern | (4) | Bach |
| (2) | Sparrow | (5) | Verdi. |
| (3) | Rose | | |

## 182
## TOM CAN PAW TAR

By repeating each word you can form a six-letter word: TOMTOM, CANCAN, PAWPAW, TARTAR.

## 183
## TRIPLETS

Assailant, Candidate, Carpentry, Forbidden, Generator, Godfather, Parsonage.

## 184
## MISSING VOWELS

| | | | |
|---|---|---|---|
| (a) | Opera | (f) | Oboe |
| (b) | Onion | (g) | Zaire |
| (c) | Ohio | (h) | Ounce |
| (d) | Idaho | (i) | Oasis |
| (e) | Ouse | (j) | Orange. |

## 185
### LINKWORDS

| | | | |
|---|---|---|---|
| (a) | Plain | (j) | Click |
| (b) | Slain | (k) | Chick |
| (c) | Stain | (l) | Thick |
| (d) | Staid | (m) | Trick |
| (e) | Stand | (n) | Trice |
| (f) | Stank | (o) | Trace |
| (g) | Stack | (p) | Trade |
| (h) | Stick | (q) | Grade |
| (i) | Slick | (r) | Glade. |

## 186
### HIDDEN COUNTRIES

| | | | |
|---|---|---|---|
| (a) | Peru | (f) | Kenya |
| (b) | Portugal | (g) | Mali |
| (c) | Chile | (h) | Uganda |
| (d) | China | (i) | Iran |
| (e) | Nepal | (j) | Benin. |

## 187
### HORSE AND CARRIAGE

| | | | |
|---|---|---|---|
| (a) | Pains | (i) | Order |
| (b) | Baggage | (j) | Main |
| (c) | Call | (k) | Cranny |
| (d) | Thrust | (l) | Circumstance |
| (e) | Fall | (m) | Nonsense |
| (f) | Loose | (n) | Feather |
| (g) | Dandy | (o) | Tide |
| (h) | Mighty | (p) | Vigour. |

## 188
### REBUS MOTTOES

(a) The understanding and overtowering mind judges between man and man.
(b) There is an overwhelming difference between vice and virtue.

## 189
### A REBUS ADDRESS

John Underwood
Andover
Hants.

## 190
### A RIOT OF REBUSES

| | | | |
|---|---|---|---|
| (a) | Roundabout | (d) | Bedspread |
| (b) | Thunderbolt | (e) | An inside job |
| (c) | A square meal | (f) | Once upon a time. |

## 191
### SHAKESPEAREAN REBUSES

(a) Much Ado About Nothing
(b) 'A little more than kin and less than kind.'

## 192
### GHOTI

The GH is pronounced as in 'enough'. The O is pronounced as in 'women'. The TI is pronounced as in 'motion'. Thus, the word is pronounced 'fish'!

## 193
### AS EASY AS ABC

| | | | |
|---|---|---|---|
| (a) | Abacus | (e) | Charabanc |
| (b) | Arabic | (f) | Abduct |
| (c) | Ambulance | (g) | Dabchick. |
| (d) | Carbolic | | |

## 194
### OFF WITH THEIR HEADS

| | | | |
|---|---|---|---|
| (a) | Lawful | (k) | Maim |
| (b) | Easter | (l) | Auntie |
| (c) | Vague | (m) | Pounce |
| (d) | Rotter | (n) | Dalliance |
| (e) | Plucky | (o) | Learned |
| (f) | Banger | (p) | Equip |
| (g) | Islander | (q) | Bovine |
| (h) | Oration | (r) | Futility |
| (i) | Pirate | (s) | Covert. |
| (j) | Hearth | | |

## 195
### MORE THAN ONE

| | | | |
|---|---|---|---|
| (a) | Teaspoonfuls | (f) | Phenomena |
| (b) | Potatoes | (g) | Oxen |
| (c) | Data | (h) | Piccolos |
| (d) | Crises | (i) | Courts-martial |
| (e) | Menservants | (j) | Mesdames. |

## 196
### SOUNDS THE SAME

| | | | |
|---|---|---|---|
| (a) | Rows; rouse | (g) | Firs; furze |
| (b) | Storey; story | (h) | Haul; hall |
| (c) | Dessert; desert | (i) | Bawl; ball |
| (d) | Site; cite | (j) | Soar; sore |
| (e) | Place; plaice | (k) | Bays; baize |
| (f) | Air; heir | (l) | Duct; ducked. |

## 197
## DOUBLETS

(a) WET, bet, bey, dey, DRY.
(b) EYE, dye, die, did, LID.
(c) OAT, rat, rot, roe, RYE.
(d) TEA, sea, set, sot, HOT.
(e) PIG, wig, wag, way, say, STY.
(f) FISH, fist, gist, girt, gird, BIRD.
(g) REST, lest, lost, loft, soft, SOFA.
(h) TEARS, sears, stars, stare, stale, stile, SMILE.
(i) POOR, boor, book, rook, rock, rick, RICH.
(j) APE, are, ere, err, ear, mar, MAN.
(k) FLOUR, floor, flood, blood, brood, broad, BREAD.
(l) MINE, mint, mist, most, moat, coat, COAL.
(m) FOUR, foul, fool, foot, fort, fore, fire, FIVE.
(n) WHEAT, cheat, cheap, cheep, creep, creed, breed, BREAD.
(o) COMB, come, home, hole, hale, hall, hail, HAIR.
(p) BLACK, blank, blink, clink, chink, chine, whine, WHITE.
(q) BREAD, break, bleak, bleat, blest, blast, boast, TOAST.
(r) TREE, free, flee, fled, feed, weed, weld, wold, WOOD.
(s) GRASS, crass, cress, tress, trees, frees, freed, greed, GREEN.
(t) ARMY, arms, aims, dims, dams, dame, name, nave, NAVY.
(u) ONE, owe, ewe, eye, dye, doe, toe, too, TWO.
(v) BLUE, glue, glut, gout, pout, port, part, pant, pint, PINK.
(w) GRUB, grab, gray, bray, brat, boat, bolt, bole, mole, mote, MOTH.
(x) RIVER, rover, cover, coves, cores, corns, coins, chins, shins, shine, shone, SHORE.
(y) WITCH, winch, wench, tench, tenth, tents, tints, tilts, tills, fills, falls, fails, fairs, FAIRY.

## 198
## ANAGRAM VERSE – 1

Vile, evil, veil, Levi, live.

## 199
## ANAGRAM VERSE – 2

Star, rats, arts, tars.

## 200
## ANAGRAM VERSE – 3

Pots, tops, stop, post.

## 201
## ABC ANAGRAMS

(a) Adroitly
(b) Alarming
(c) Aridness
(d) Adherent
(e) Alignment
(f) Ascension
(g) Antagonist
(h) Abhorrent
(i) Brigade
(j) Butchers
(k) Bordello
(l) Bacterial
(m) Bargained
(n) Bestarred
(o) Blessing
(p) Bestiary
(q) Crumpets
(r) Consigned
(s) Calumnies
(t) Catechism
(u) Coastline
(v) Colonialist
(w) Containerised
(x) Coalitionist.

## 202
## THE END

(a) Bathe
(b) Loathe
(c) Seethe
(d) Lethe
(e) Blithe
(f) Writhe
(g) Clothe
(h) Soothe
(i) Breathe
(j) Scythe.

## 203
## THE BEGINNING

(a) Theatre
(b) Thesaurus
(c) Thermometer
(d) Thebes
(e) Theodolite
(f) Thermal
(g) Theta
(h) Thermidor
(i) Thespian
(j) Themis.

## 204
## SOUNDS BEASTLY

| | | | |
|---|---|---|---|
| (a) | Bare, bear | (i) | Turn, tern |
| (b) | Be, bee | (j) | Links, lynx |
| (c) | Dear, deer | (k) | Rough, ruff |
| (d) | Flee, flea | (l) | Soul, sole |
| (e) | Bore, boar | (m) | Towed, toad |
| (f) | Hoarse, horse | (n) | Mewl, mule |
| (g) | Hair, hare | (o) | Lune, loon. |
| (h) | Lama, llama | | |

## 205
## AMERICAN ENGLISH

| | | | |
|---|---|---|---|
| (a) | Suspenders | (h) | Zip code |
| (b) | Cotton candy | (i) | Stroller |
| (c) | Slingshot | (j) | Desk clerk |
| (d) | Lobby | (k) | Salesclerk |
| (e) | Period | (l) | Candy store |
| (f) | Popsicle | (m) | Closet |
| (g) | Diaper | (n) | Windshield. |

## 206
## TWO IN ONE

| | | | |
|---|---|---|---|
| (a) | Smart | (g) | Craft |
| (b) | Tie | (h) | Line |
| (c) | Lean | (i) | Brood |
| (d) | Spring | (j) | Sound |
| (e) | Leave | (k) | End |
| (f) | Close | (l) | Temper. |

## 207
## FIND THE BIRDS

| | | | |
|---|---|---|---|
| (a) | Starling | (h) | Turnstone |
| (b) | Whinchat | (i) | Razorbill |
| (c) | Yellowhammer | (j) | Swallow |
| (d) | Goshawk | (k) | Redstart |
| (e) | Wheatear | (l) | Redwing |
| (f) | Peregrine | (m) | Nuthatch |
| (g) | Dotterel | (n) | Siskin. |

## 208
## A SHORT VOCABULARY TEST

(a) A three-toed sloth.
(b) A heavy Burmese knife.
(c) A river or running water.
(d) A kind of violin used in Shetland.
(e) A sweetheart.
(f) A double, or genius.
(g) A Chinese unit of distance.
(h) A supposed force manifested in magnetism, hypnotism, etc.
(i) Precious jade.
(j) The male of a sort of Himalayan cattle.

## 209
## FOUR OF A KIND

| | | | |
|---|---|---|---|
| (a) | Teepee | (f) | Riffraff |
| (b) | Voodoo | (g) | Gagging |
| (c) | Assess | (h) | Statuette |
| (d) | Cannoning | (i) | Maharaja |
| (e) | Diddled | (j) | Razzmatazz. |

There may be alternative answers.

## 210
## MEANINGFUL NAMES

| | | | |
|---|---|---|---|
| (a) | Moustached | (f) | Laugh |
| (b) | Bright raven | (g) | Bee |
| (c) | White breast | (h) | Lover of horses |
| (d) | Sunday | (i) | Noose |
| (e) | World chief | (j) | Little she-bear. |

## 211
## ANIMAL ADJECTIVES

| | | | |
|---|---|---|---|
| (a) | Hawks | (g) | Wolves |
| (b) | Snakes | (h) | Mice |
| (c) | Geese | (i) | Sheep |
| (d) | Goats | (j) | Peacocks |
| (e) | Deer | (k) | Bears |
| (f) | Lizards | (l) | Foxes. |

## 212
## WORD MIX

1 Queuing (or cooeeing)
2 Bookkeeper
3 Strengths
4 Uncopyrightable (or misconjugatedly)
5 Feedback and boldface.

## 213
## A COLLECTION OF COLLECTIVES

| | | | |
|---|---|---|---|
| (a) | Murmuration | (k) | Congregation |
| (b) | Clowder | (l) | Covey |
| (c) | Kindle | (m) | Leap |
| (d) | Cete | (n) | Knot |
| (e) | Parliament | (o) | Rafter |
| (f) | Shrewdness | (p) | Crash |
| (g) | Ostentation | (q) | Pod |
| (h) | Watch | (r) | Mustering |
| (i) | Skulk | (s) | Husk |
| (j) | Unkindness | (t) | Murder. |

## 214
## A SIMPLE CHARADE

Tar-get.

## 215
## THE ARAB SHEPHERD

Lamplight (lamb-plight).

## 216
## BESIDE THE BROOK

Crescent (cress-scent).

## 217
## VERY FEMININE

Was-her-woman.

## 218
## A SYLVAN CHARADE

Bull-rush.

## 219
## A SPARKLING PUZZLE

SPARKLING, SPARKING, SPARING, SPRING, SPRIG, PRIG, PIG, PI, I.

## 220
## A BURIED QUOTATION

The quality of mercy is not strained.

## 221
## MORE MISSING WORDS

SPRITE, STRIPE, RIPEST, PRIEST.

## 222
## YET MORE MISSING WORDS

DEARTH, THREAD, DARETH, HATRED.

## 223
## AN ANGLING PASTIME

In addition to the two examples given you should have been able to land the following fish: perch, roach, bream, sprat, ling, carp, tench, herring, dace, sole, barbel, whiting, swordfish, trout, chub, salmon.

## 224
## HIDDEN FRUITS

The twelve fruits, in order, are: fig, date, apple, peach, nectarine, melon, pear, orange, olive, gourd, lemon and raisin.

## 225
## THE EXCURSION

The missing words are: noon, eve, Bob, Hannah, pop, peep, ewe, dad, tit, Aha, sees, eye, pup, keek, bib, pap, tot, deified, pip, nun, redder, tut, did, madam, deed, refer, level, eke, poop, oho, reviver, mum, gag, toot, civic, sexes, tenet.

## 226
## BUILDING A WORD SQUARE

The letters can be arranged as follows:

| | | | | | |
|---|---|---|---|---|---|
| P | A | S | T | O | R |
| A | T | T | I | R | E |
| S | T | U | P | I | D |
| T | I | P | T | O | E |
| O | R | I | O | L | E |
| R | E | D | E | E | M |

## 227
## COMPLETE THE WORD SQUARE

```
N  E  S  T  L  E  S
E  N  T  R  A  N  T
S  T  R  A  N  G  E
T  R  A  I  T  O  R
L  A  N  T  E  R  N
E  N  G  O  R  G  E
S  T  E  R  N  E  R
```

## 228
## THE FIRST PUBLISHED DOUBLE ACROSTIC

### The Words
London's the 'world in little'; 'make a note on't,'
Thames it is – cesspool; 'that's the long and short on't.'

### The Letters
At State receptions in day's untaxed *Light*,
Are *Ostrich* plumes a fair and goodly sight.
The *Neva* with old Thames will never cope,
Though *Despotism* dwell in Naples soap.
As for poor Cook? *O-why-hee* must excuse
The tale of his sad fate; 'tis now no *News*.

```
L  i  g  h              T
O  s  t  r  i  c         H
N  e        v           A
D  e  s  p  o  t  i  s   M
O  -  w  h  y  -  h  e   E
N        e     w        S
```

## 229
## QUEEN VICTORIA'S ACROSTIC

| N | aple    | S |
| E | lb      | E |
| W | ashingto | N |
| C | incinnat | I |
| A | msterda | M |
| S | tambou  | L |
| T | orne    | A |
| L | epant   | O |
| E | clipti  | C |

## 230
## AN ENGLISHMAN

| J | o     | B |
| O | rmol  | U |
| H | ande  | L |
| N | arwha | L |

## 231
## A LEWIS CARROLL ACROSTIC

| Q | uadrati | C |
| U | nderg   | O |
| A | lar     | M |
| S | trea    | M |
| I | c       | E |
| I | nteri   | M |
| N |         | O |
| S | uppe    | R |
| A | ren     | A |
| N | igh     | T |
| I |         | I |
| T | w       | O |
| Y | aw      | N |

## 232
## A CRYPTIC ACROSTIC

| C | y | n | i | C |
| O | p | e | r | A |
| N | y | l | o | N |
| S | e | p | i | A |
| T | i | d | a | L |
| A | m | b | l | E |
| B | e | a | s | T |
| L | e | a | s | T |
| E | r | a | t | O |

## 233
### THE FIRST CROSSWORD

## 234
### THE SECOND CROSSWORD

## 235
### A D-DAY CROSSWORD

*Across:* 1. LONG ISLAND 8. IDLE 10. DEMOCRATIC 11. RUIN 12. EDGE 15. NEW YORK 18. ALICE 19. ERECT 20. BREVE 21. INGOT 22. POSER 23. UNION 24. GREEN 25. USHER 26. EARNEST 30. PELT 33. PROS 34. WATERTIGHT 35. KIWI 36. GARDEN GATE
*Down:* 2. OMEN 3. GLOVE 4. SURLY 5. ACTOR 6. DICE 7. FLAG 9. BREAKING UP 10. DIVING BELL 13. DRESS-SHIRT 14. ENTERPRISE 15. NEPTUNE 16. OCEAN 17. KEEP OUT 20. BRIAR 27. ASTER 28. NORSE 29. SLING 31. EVIL 32. TWIG 33. PHUT

## 236
### STANDARD CRYPTIC – 1

*Across:* 1. ORCHARDS 5. LAMMAS 9. CONTENTS 10. STODGE 11. LANDLORD 12. ARTIST 14. BEAR WITH ME 18. SAMARITANS 22. ALLEGE 23. SYCAMORE 24. LAIRDS 25. INFORMAL 26. DANISH 27. APPENDIX
*Down:* 1. OCCULT 2. CANONS 3. AGE-OLD 4. DETERGENTS 6. ASTEROID 7. MIDNIGHT 8. SHEATHED 13. BRANDY SNAP 15. ASSAILED 16. EMULSION 17. BRIGADES 19. LAHORE 20. FORMED 21. REFLEX

## 237
### STANDARD CRYPTIC – 2

*Across:* 1. LOW-GRADE 5. STENCH 9. BIGAMIST 10. UNISON 12. CANON 13. BAR-TENDER 14. FLAGON 16. TRIFLES 19. OUTLAST 21. AVENUE 23. CHRISTMAS 25. ORDER 26. REASON 27. INTEREST 28. EASTER 29. CLEANSER
*Down:* 1. LUBECK 2. WAGONS-LIT 3. ROMAN 4. DUSTBIN 6. TANGERINE 7. NOSED 8. HUNTRESS 11. TROT 15. GLADSTONE 17. LAUNDRESS 18. CONCORDE 20. TOME 21. ARSENAL 22. GRATER 24. ROAMS 25. OPERA

## 238
### ANAGRAM CROSSWORD

*Across:* 1. DISBAR  4. STASIS  8.
SAPIENT  10. WIRED  11. SPRIG  12.
SERVANT  13. VERSATILE  17.
ABRIDGE  19. NOTES  21. GROAN  22.
TORPEDO  23. RUSTED  24. ADHERE
*Down:* 1. DISUSE  2. SUPER  3.
AVENGER  5. TOWER  6. SURNAME  7.
SEDATE  9. TESTAMENT  13.
VARIOUS  14. IGNORED  15.
DANGER  16. ASHORE  18. DENSE  20.
THESE

## 239
### PRINTER'S DEVILRY

| | | | | | |
|---|---|---|---|---|---|
| A | R | T | I | S | T | R | Y |

Grid:
```
A R T I S T R Y
S O R E A G U E
S A A R M A D A
A R I D E L E R
U D N U R U I N
L I S S O M C I
T R E E A N O N
S T A R T I N G
```

Here's where the breaks come in the Printer's
Devilry clues:

1. ap/ing  7. l/ady  8. te/sts  9. l/ily-maid
11. b/read  14. Pe/ter  16. b/it  17. mi/nd
18. r/emember  19. divine/r

## 240
### GIVE AND TAKE

Here are the correct forms of the words that were
misprinted:

*Across:* 1. Tax  4. Fan  9. Residue  10.
Cooked  11. Wards  12. Wave  13. Meal  15.
Plumes  18. Snail  20. Slave  23. Resident  24.
Twin  26. Swallow  27. Law  28.
Game-birds  29. Rough
*Down:* 1. Stored  2. Cats  3. Bogs  4. Pain  5.
Stories  6. Rum  7. Rills  8. Clause  14.
Mount  16. Hair  17. Plain  19. Grub  21.
Comic  22. Flying  23. Equip  25. Riata

| B | O | U | J | N | F | U | B | C | P | M | F |
|---|---|---|---|---|---|---|---|---|---|---|---|
| Z | Q | F | H | U | D | H | M | S | Z | J | D |
| Q | Z | R | O | T | M | Z | Q | F | T | U | M |
| Q | F | O | O | F | S | M | T | S | L | D | F |
| H | T | T | D | V | N | C | B | F | R | I | D |
| V | D | M | C | X | N | N | J | T | G | J | U |
| H | S | F | B | W | F | I | C | Q | H | M | J |
| S | F | D | G | N | U | F | Y | P | O | J | D |
| B | D | Q | H | R | D | D | P | S | O | F | B |
| G | P | T | U | Z | M | V | T | U | N | C | M |
| D | V | T | D | V | T | C | S | B | A | J | M |
| S | Q | Z | C | D | R | B | Z | M | S | H | Z |

| C | A | D | A | V | E | R | M | I | M | I | C |
|---|---|---|---|---|---|---|---|---|---|---|---|
| O | X | I | D | E | B | E | A | T | E | N | R |
| N | E | G | A | T | E | S | T | E | A | D | Y |
| S | D | E | P | O | S | I | T | M | T | I | P |
| E | R | S | T | C | O | D | E | Y | H | A | T |
| R | E | T | E | S | S | E | R | A | E | N | O |
| V | E | L | D | T | O | N | T | W | A | N | G |
| A | L | E | D | I | S | C | E | N | D | O | R |
| T | E | N | I | N | T | E | N | T | A | V | A |
| O | R | N | A | T | E | S | E | E | R | I | P |
| R | S | I | L | E | N | T | M | A | T | C | H |
| Y | I | E | L | D | O | D | Y | S | S | E | Y |

*Across:* 1. antimetabole   9. Argive (car given)   10. intake (key)   12. slypes   14. penner   15. nutmeg (rev.)   16. scum (SCM)   18. Wendy   19. misfit   20. greave (Jimmy Greaves)   25. drink   29. exon   30. cerise   31. cornea   32. stylus   33. cus(-)cus   34. brazil (lizard)   35. Tradescantia

*Down:* 1. carriwitchet   2. Prague (anag. & lit.)   3. kipped (PE)   4. Gentoo   5. viand (i in van (3) + d & lit.)   6. breres   7. litchi   8. eclectically   11. spunge   13. ruck (2 mngs)   17. shippo   21. recoup (Cu)   22. chived   23. Xosa   24. Hecuba   26. portal (Al)   27. Liebig (*L*, abbr.)   28. Venus (Ve + sun (rev.) & lit.)

The first four clues written by Sir Leonard led to negate (ne-gat-e), tesserae (anag.), Endor (end + or) and so-so (S.O.S. + O) and the fifth was the devious indication of where to look for the murderer. It led to the word 'diagram' (aid (rev.) + gram), which told the Inspector to look not at the puzzle, but at the bars which separated the words. These bars are in the shape of Lucius I. Feisthill, whom he promptly and correctly arrested.

## 243
### A CROSSWORD BY SIR MAX BEERBOHM

If you have completed this crossword, then you have achieved the impossible!

When Sir Max submitted this crossword to *The Times* it was accompanied by this letter:

> No doubt you, like most people, have sometimes thought of some utterly awful thing that you *could* do if you chose to, some disastrous and devastating thing the very thought of which has brought cold sweat to your brow? And you may have at some time thought: 'Suppose I released into the columns of *The Times*, one of these fine days, a crossword puzzle with clues signifying nothing whatsoever,' and may have hideously pictured to yourself the effect on all educated parts of Great Britain? You may incidentally have seen yourself going into your club shortly before luncheon time and observing in the armchairs men with blank, set, fixed, pale, just-not-despairing faces, poring over the current issue? – one of them perhaps rising unsteadily and lumbering out to the library and asking the librarian, 'Have we a Wordsworth concordance?' – or some question of that sort. You may have figured this man going home at teatime, and his wife saying, 'Oh, Stephen, is anything the matter?' He: 'No, dear, nothing.' She: 'But you look so pale. You . . .' He: 'I've had a rather hard day, dear. But I'm quite all right.'
>
> And you may further have wondered just how the apology in next day's issue should be worded – just what excuse should be offered, before the shutters in Printing House Square were briskly and slammingly put up for ever?
>
> Perhaps I oughtn't to remind you of this nightmare of yours. Forgive me.
>
> P.S. The nightmare wouldn't be loathsomely complete unless a few of the clues were quite genuine – *and very simple*, so as to put the solvers in good heart, and make them confident of success, and keep their shoulders to the wheel. I have provided six such clues, with my usual forethought.

*The Times* did publish this crossword, but rather spoilt the effect by printing the letter alongside!

## 244
### CROSS-REFERENCE

1 = O,  2 = B,  3 = J,  4 = E,  5 = C,  6 = T,  7 = F,  8 = L,  9 = W,  10 = R,  11 = S,  12 = H,  13 = Q,  14 = X,  15 = D,  16 = A,  17 = N,  18 = K,  19 = I,  20 = G,  21 = V,  22 = P,  23 = Z,  24 = Y,  25 = U,  26 = M.

## 245
### ELIMINATOR PUZZLE

*Across:* 1. OPPOSITE  2. AMNESIA  3. REGION  4. SILHOUETTE  5. FLEET  6. JEOPARDY  7. IGNORANT  8. VOYAGER  9. ZEPHYR  10. QUARREL  11. FORBIDDEN  12. PATRON  13. UNWED  *Down:* 1. WOMAN  2. DUBIOUS  3. HARMONY  4. GAINSAY  5. JAUNT  6. GRIMY  7. FUNCTION  8. HUMBUG  9. COLOUR  10. DAILY  11. BOUGH  12. COUPLE  13. CLIMB.

## 246
### CRYPTIC WORD SEARCH

1. DEAL (b15–e12)  2. HULL (i11–l14)  3. YORK (n11–k8)  4. DOVER (m12–i8)  5. STOKE (n5–j9)  6. EPSOM (a4–e8)  7. BLYTH (a5–a9)  8. NEWARK (f12–k7)  9. TOTNES (j1–o1)  10. REDCAR (j4–e4)  11. ILFORD (d1–d6)  12. OLDHAM (o2–o7)  13. JARROW (n15–i15)  14. SIDCUP (b10–b5)  15. REDRUTH (a15–a9)  16. WALSALL (i15–o9)  17. BURSLEM (k2–e2)  18. BAKEWELL (o15–o8)  19. MINEHEAD (e15–l8)  20. CARLISLE (h7–a14)  21. ROCHDALE (f9–f2)  22. RAMSGATE (n8–n1)  23. FLEETWOOD (f1–n9)  24. LANCASTER (o3–g3)  25. MORECAMBE (b3–j11)  26. BARNSTAPLE (l10–c1)  27. ALTRINCHAM (l13–c13)  28. DARLINGTON (d12–m3)  29. SUNDERLAND (g15–g6)  30. FOLKESTONE (c11–c2)

## 247
### HONEYCOMB

1. METEOR  2. MOTETS  3. MINUTE  4. PSALMS  5. TULIPS  6. LUNATE  7. CEASED  8. PISCES  9. SILENT  10. THRONE  11. DECIDE  12. STATIC  13. NOUGAT  14. EDITOR  15. DOTAGE  16. RODENT.

## 248
## UP AND DOWN

He is not tall enough to reach the button for the eighteenth floor.

## 249
## BEAR FACTS

For the explorer to find himself back at his camp after walking as indicated, his camp must have been at the North Pole. Therefore the bear must have been a polar bear, and so its colour was white.

## 250
## EIGHT COINS

Put three coins on one side of the balance and three on the other. Either the scales will balance (showing the counterfeit to be among the three not on the balance) or one side of the balance will be higher (showing the counterfeit to be among the three on that side).

Take whichever group of three contains the counterfeit. Weigh any two of these coins, one against the other. Either the scales will balance (identifying the counterfeit as the one not on the scales) or one side will be higher (thus identifying the counterfeit as being the coin on that side).

## 251
## TWENTY-EIGHT DAYS

All months have twenty-eight days (and most have a few more).

## 252
## PRO OR ANTI?

Agreement.

## 253
## CONTINUE THE SERIES

N, T. The letters are the initial letters of the numbers one, two, three, four, etc.

## 254
## THREE CARDS

The Ace of Hearts, the Queen of Spades, the Seven of Diamonds.

## 255
## TRUE AND FALSE

Statement (e).

## 256
## SONG CONTEST

*First:* Jean, the Belgian, singing 'Non Plus'.
*Second:* Pierre, the Frenchman, singing 'C'est La Vie'. *Third:* Louis, the Swiss, singing 'Quelque Chose'.

## 257
## TOSSING A COIN

The probability that Bill will win is 2/3.

## 258
## DAYS IN A DAZE

Thursday.

## 259
## TOM, DICK AND HARRY

Tom must always drink gin. Dick must always drink whisky. So Harry is the only one who might sometimes drink gin and sometimes whisky.

## 260
## FLATMATES

It must have been Sharon who wore Sally's earrings and Susan's necklace. Therefore Sally must have worn Sharon's necklace.

## 261
## MISSIONARIES AND CANNIBALS

Call the three missionaries M, m, m, and the three cannibals C, c, c – the capital letters denoting the missionary and the cannibal who can row the boat. Then:

C, c row across;
C returns with the boat;
C, c row across;
C returns;
M, m row across;
M, c return;
M, C row across;
M, c return;
M, m row across;
C returns;
C, c row across;
C returns;
C, c row across.

## 262
## THREE JEALOUS HUSBANDS

Call the three men A, B, C and their wives a, b, c. Then:

A, a row across;
A returns;
b, c row across;
b returns;
A, C row across;
A, a return;
A, B row across;
c returns;
b, c row across;
A returns;
A, a row across.

## 263
## THE ISLAND OF TRU-LI – 1

When asked, 'Are you a Trui or a Lia?' any native of Tru-Li must reply, 'I am a Trui' – Truis because this is the truth, and Lias because they will tell lies about being Lias. Therefore we cannot tell whether the native in the distance was a Trui or a Lia, but the messenger must be a Trui.

## 264
## THE ISLAND OF TRU-LI – 2

B must have lied when he said A claimed to be a Lia, and A must have told the truth when he said that B lied. So A is a Trui and B is a Lia.

## 265
## THE ISLAND OF TRU-LI – 3

There are four possibilities: C and D are both Truis; C is a Trui and D is a Lia; C and D are both Lias; C is a Lia and D is a Trui. In the first case the statement would be false, so C, being a Trui, could not make it. In the other cases, the statement would be true, so it could not be made by a Lia. Therefore the only possible solution is that C is a Trui and D a Lia.

## 266
## THE ISLAND OF TRU-LI – 4

In this case, C and D must both be Lias.

## 267
## THE ISLAND OF TRU-LI – 5

Pointing at either road, he should say to either of the natives, 'If I were to ask you if this is the way I should go, would your answer be yes?' This should elicit the correct answer, whether the native be a Trui or a Lia.

## 268
## A GAME OF WHIST

Pat is the hairdresser, Chris the teacher, Lee the journalist, and Kit the estate agent.

## 269
## A STRAIGHTFORWARD QUESTION

The question is equivalent to this: 'If the puzzle you solved before you solved this one was easier than this one, was the puzzle you solved before you solved this one easier than this one?'
Obviously, the answer must be YES!

## 270
## MARKS FOR LOGIC

The successful applicant reasoned thus. Since all three of us raised our hands, there are only two possibilities: two red marks and one green, or three red marks. If my mark is green, either of the others would see one red and one green, and therefore would quickly be able to deduce that his own was red. Since that has not happened, each of the others must see two red marks. Therefore all the marks are red, including my own.

## 271
## THE COMMITTEE

John is the secretary, Luke is the chairman, Matthew is the vice-chairman, Mark is the treasurer.

## 272
## KING ARTHUR'S KNIGHTS

On the second evening King Arthur arranged the knights and himself in the following order round the table: A, F, B, D, G, E, C. On the third evening they sat thus: A, E, B, G, C, F, D. He thus had B next but one to him on both occasions (the nearest possible) and G was the third from him at both sittings (the furthest position possible). No other way of seating the knights would have been so satisfactory.

## 273
## FOUR LADIES

Rose Sayers earns the most. Olive Marsh is the market analyst. Hazel and Olive live 4 miles apart.

The steps toward the solution can be summarized as follows: Ivy must be Miss James. Rose must be Miss Sayers. The research chemist must be Hazel. Olive must be Miss Marsh. Hazel must be Miss Christie. Ivy James must be the optician. Rose Sayers can't be the market analyst, so Olive Marsh must be. Rose Sayers must be the archaeologist. The distance between Hazel and Olive is worked out with the help of good old Pythagoras.

## 274
## A DINNER-PARTY

Mr Stevenson was immediately to the left of his father-in-law. So his father-in-law can't be Johnson, who was next but one to him; nor Edmundson nor Richardson, who both sat between two ladies. So the father-in-law must be Thompson.

Label the positions round the table 1 to 10, and call Mr Thompson 1 and Mr Stevenson 2. Mrs Stevenson, next but one to Mr Thompson, must be at 9, otherwise she would be next to her husband. Mr Johnson, next but one to Mr Stevenson, must be at 4, otherwise three men would be together and it would not be possible to have three of the ladies each sitting between two men.

For the same reason, positions 6 and 8 must be occupied by Edmundson and Richardson (though we don't yet know in which order). For Mrs Johnson to sit next to her sister, she must be at 10. Mrs Richardson, next but two to her, must be at 3 (not 7, as this would put her next to her husband). The rest is easy.

The seating arrangements are therefore as follows, in clockwise sequence: Mr Thompson, Mr Stevenson, Mrs Richardson, Mr Johnson, Mrs Edmundson, Mr Richardson, Mrs Thompson, Mr Edmundson, Mrs Stevenson, Mrs Johnson.

## 275
## LEWIS CARROLL'S SYMBOLIC LOGIC – 1

No engine-driver lives on barley-sugar.

## 276
## SYMBOLIC LOGIC – 2

I cannot read any of Brown's letters.

## 277
## SYMBOLIC LOGIC – 3

I always avoid a kangaroo.

## 278
## TWELVE COINS

Number the coins from 1 to 12. Weigh 1, 2, 3 and 4 against 5, 6, 7 and 8.

If they balance, weigh 1 and 9 against 10 and 11 (we now know that 1 is a genuine coin). If they balance, 12 must be the counterfeit and by weighing it against a coin known to be genuine we can determine whether it is heavy or light. If 1 and 9 do not balance against 10 and 11, then for the third weighing weigh 10 against 11. If 1 and 9 were heavier than 10 and 11, the result of the third weighing will tell whether 9 is heavy, 10 is light or 11 is light. If 1 and 9 were lighter than 10 and 11, the result of the third weighing will tell whether 9 is light, 10 is heavy or 11 is heavy.

If, on the first weighing, 1, 2, 3 and 4 are heavier than 5, 6, 7 and 8, this means either that one of 1, 2, 3, 4 is heavy or one of 5, 6, 7, 8 is light. Weigh 1, 2 and 5 against 3, 6 and 9. If they balance, weigh 7 against 8 – this will determine whether 4 is heavy or 7 is light or 8 is light. If 1, 2 and 5 are heavier than 3, 6 and 9, weigh 1 against 2. This will determine whether 6 is light or 1 is heavy or 2 is heavy. If 1, 2 and 5 are lighter than 3, 6 and 9, weigh 1 against 5 – this will determine whether 3 is heavy or 5 is light.

If, on the first weighing, 1, 2, 3 and 4 are lighter than 5, 6, 7 and 8, carry out the same weighings as in the previous paragraph. This time the results will show (a) whether 4 is light or 7 is heavy or 8 is heavy, or (b) whether 6 is heavy or 1 is light or 2 is light, or (c) whether 3 is light or 5 is heavy.

## 279
## HOW MANY TRIANGLES?

There are thirty-five triangles.

## 280
## A FLOWER BED

The flower bed is 15 feet (4.6 metres) long and 9 feet (2.7 metres) wide.

## 281
## TRACE IT

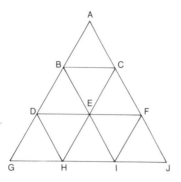

There are several solutions, e.g. start from H and take the following route: H, G, B, E, C, B, A, F, E, I, F, J, H, E, D, H.

## 282
## THE CARDBOARD BOX

The areas of the top and side multiplied together and divided by the area of the end give the square of the length. Similarly, the product of top and end divided by side gives the square of the length; and the product of side and end divided by the top gives the square of the depth.

We need to perform only one of these operations. Thus 240 multiplied by 300 divided by 180 gives 400. Hence the length is 20. The width and the depth, therefore, must be 12 and 15 respectively.

## 283
## HOW LONG IS THE DIAGONAL?

Is AB is 5, then CD is also 5. CE is therefore 10. But CE is a radius of the circle, and so is the diagonal BC. So BC is 10, and the other diagonal AD must be the same length. Therefore the length of the diagonal AD is 10.

## 284
## THE PAINTED CUBE

(a) 8    (b) 12    (c) 6    (d) 1

## 285
## HOW TO DRAW AN OVAL

If you place your sheet of paper round the surface of a cylindrical bottle or canister, the oval can be drawn with one sweep of the compasses.

## 286
## A SPHERICAL BALLOON

From the formulae for the surface and volume of a sphere ($d^2$ *pi* and $d^3$ *pi*/6, respectively) it is easy to work out that the diameter of the balloon must be 6 inches, giving a surface area of 36 *pi* square inches and a volume of 36 *pi* cubic inches.

## 287
## BUYING ASPARAGUS

Both were wrong, and the lady was badly cheated. She only got half the quantity that would be contained in the large bundle, and therefore should have been charged half the original price. A circle with a circumference half that of another must have its area a quarter that of the other.

## 288
## CUTTING A RING

Nine pieces.

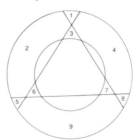

## 289
## THE ARTIST'S CANVAS

The canvas must be 10 inches (25 cm) wide and 20 inches (51 cm) high. The picture itself will be 6 inches (15 cm) wide and 12 inches (30 cm) high, and the margins will be as required.

## 290
## THE LADDER

When the bottom of the ladder was pulled out, a right-angled triangle was formed with base 11 feet, height $4x$ feet and hypotenuse $5x$ feet.

$16x^2 + 121 = 25x^2$
So $x^2 = 121/9$
So $5x = 55/3$

Therefore the length of the ladder is $55/3$ feet or 18 feet 4 inches.

## 291
## SPHERES ROUND A SPHERE

Six.

## 292
## THE CLOTHES-LINE PUZZLE

The height of the intersection is obtained by dividing the product of the heights of the posts by the sum of the heights of the posts, i.e. $(a \times b)/(a + b)$. In this particular case the answer is $^{35}/_{12}$ or 2 feet 11 inches (89 cm).

It is interesting that the answer is not dependent on how far the poles are apart. If you thought this information was necessary to solve the puzzle, you might like to work out why this is not so.

## 293
## A TANK PUZZLE

When the first cube is put in, the water rises 1.8 inches (4.6 cm). When the second cube is put in, the water rises another 2.2 inches (5.6 cm).

## 294
## STEALING THE BELL-ROPES

Whenever we have one side (a) of a right-angled triangle, and know the difference between the second side and the hypotenuse (which difference we will call b), then the length of the hypotenuse will be $\frac{a^2}{2b} + \frac{b}{2}$. In the case of our puzzle this will be $\frac{48^2}{6} + 1\frac{1}{2}$ inches. Therefore the length of the rope will be 32 feet 1½ inches.

## 295
## RECTANGLE TO SQUARE – 1

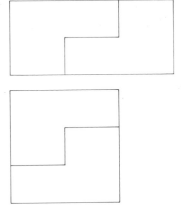

## 296
## RECTANGLE TO SQUARE – 2

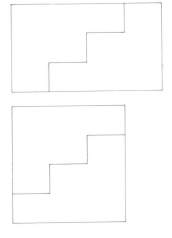

## 297
## RECTANGLE TO SQUARE – 3

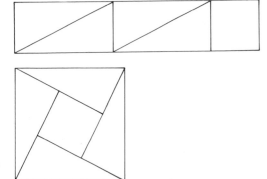

## 298
## TWO SQUARES TO ONE

Measure off ab equal to cd, then cut as shown.

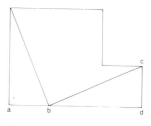

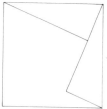

## 299
## A GREEK CROSS DISSECTION

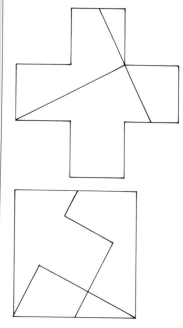

## 300
## SQUARE TO GREEK CROSSES

Mark out the square into twenty-five smaller squares, and then cut as shown.

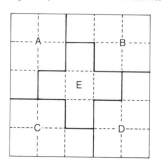

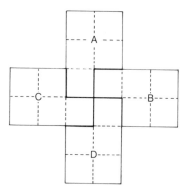

## 301
## QUADRUPLICATION

Mark off the figure into twelve equal triangles, and then cut as indicated.

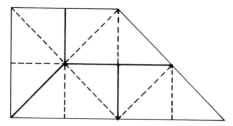

## 302
### THE SPHINX

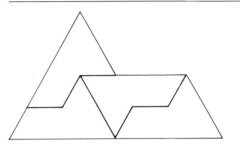

## 303
### TWO FIELDS

The square field is 3363 yards square (perimeter 13,452, area 11,309,769).

The rectangular field is 2378 by 4756 yards (perimeter 14,268, area 11,309,768).

## 304
### THE SEMI-CIRCULAR ISLAND

Approximately 157½ square miles.

## 305
### A UNIQUE SPHERE

$4r^2$ must lie between 1000 and 9999. Hence $50 > r > 15$. $\frac{4r^3}{3}$ also lies between 1000 and 9999, hence $20 > r > 9$. Therefore r must be 16, 17, 18, or 19. But for $\frac{4r^3}{3}$ to be an integer, r must be a multiple of 3.

Therefore the radius of the sphere is 18, giving an area of 1296 *pi* and a volume of 7776 *pi*.

## 306
### COUNTING THE RECTANGLES

There are 1296 different rectangles in all, 204 of which are squares.

## 307
### A ROUND-THE-WORLD WALK

Approximately 37.6992 feet (11.5 metres).

## 308
### SHOWBIZ

(a)  Frank Sinatra      (d)  Marlon Brando
(b)  Gracie Fields      (e)  Alfred Hitchcock
(c)  Noel Coward        (f)  James Dean.

## 309
### CRIMINAL CONNECTIONS

(a)  Ian Fleming          (f)  Raymond Chandler
(b)  G. K. Chesterton     (g)  Agatha Christie
(c)  P. D. James          (h)  Leslie Charteris
(d)  Arthur Conan Doyle   (i)  John Le Carré
(e)  Georges Simenon      (j)  Dorothy L. Sayers.

## 310
### THE YOUNG ONES

(a)  Cub        (f)  Elver
(b)  Gosling    (g)  Pup
(c)  Fawn       (h)  Calf
(d)  Kid        (i)  Leveret
(e)  Cygnet     (j)  Squab.

## 311
### MONEY, MONEY, MONEY

(a)  Greece        (d)  Austria
(b)  Spain         (e)  Portugal
(c)  Yugoslavia    (f)  Ireland.

## 312
### WHAT THE DICKENS?

(a)  David Copperfield
(b)  A Tale Of Two Cities
(c)  The Pickwick Papers
(d)  Oliver Twist
(e)  Martin Chuzzlewit
(f)  Nicholas Nickleby.

## 313
### GILBERT AND SULLIVAN

(a)  shreds, patches
(b)  maids, school
(c)  elliptical billiard balls
(d)  modern Major-General
(e)  constabulary, policeman
(f)  curate
(g)  elderly ugly daughter
(h)  cook, captain, mate.

## 314
### DATES

(a)  February 14    (d)  November 30
(b)  April 23       (e)  March 1.
(c)  March 17

## 315
## LAND-LOCKED

You could have chosen any 20 from these 29:
Andorra, Austria, Czechoslovakia, Hungary, Liechtenstein, Luxembourg, San Marino, Switzerland, Afghanistan, Bhutan, Laos, Mongolia, Nepal, Bolivia, Paraguay, Burkina Faso, Burundi, Chad, Central African Republic, Botswana, Lesotho, Malawi, Mali, Niger, Rwanda, Swaziland, Uganda, Zambia, Zimbabwe.

## 316
## STATES

Alabama, Alaska, Arizona, California, Florida, Georgia, Indiana, Iowa, Louisiana, Minnesota, Montana, Nebraska, Nevada, North Carolina, North Dakota, Oklahoma, Pennsylvania, South Carolina, South Dakota, Virginia, West Virginia.

## 317
## FIRST NAMES FIRST

| | | | |
|---|---|---|---|
| (a) | Pablo | (f) | Gustav |
| (b) | Ludwig | (g) | Henri |
| (c) | Vincent | (h) | Antonio |
| (d) | Edward | (i) | Albrecht |
| (e) | Edwin | (j) | Frederick. |

## 318
## OUT OF TOWN

| | | | |
|---|---|---|---|
| (a) | 118 | (f) | 405 |
| (b) | 53 | (g) | 135 |
| (c) | 120 | (h) | 564 |
| (d) | 307 | (i) | 212 |
| (e) | 78 | (j) | 209. |

## 319
## AUTHORS A TO Z

| | |
|---|---|
| (a) | John Steinbeck |
| (b) | George Orwell |
| (c) | W. M. Thackeray |
| (d) | E. M. Forster |
| (e) | Jerome K. Jerome |
| (f) | Jules Verne |
| (g) | Boris Pasternak |
| (h) | Grace Metalious |
| (i) | Stephen Crane |
| (j) | J. P. Donleavy |
| (k) | Philip Roth |
| (l) | Leon Uris |
| (m) | Richard Llewellyn |
| (n) | Beryl Bainbridge |
| (o) | Jeffrey Archer |
| (p) | Christopher Isherwood |
| (q) | Nikos Kazantzakis |
| (r) | Émile Zola |
| (s) | Evelyn Waugh |
| (t) | Ellery Queen |
| (u) | Robert Heinlein |
| (v) | Maria Edgeworth |
| (w) | William Golding |
| (x) | Vladimir Nabokov |
| (y) | Frank Yerby. |

## 320
## FOR LATIN LOVERS

| | |
|---|---|
| (a) | sound of mind |
| (b) | an essential condition |
| (c) | a slip of the tongue |
| (d) | with stronger reason |
| (e) | in the commission of the crime |
| (f) | healthy mind in healthy body |
| (g) | beyond powers or rights conferred by law |
| (h) | without a day being appointed |
| (i) | after the deed is done |
| (j) | to the point |
| (k) | one thing for another, tit for tat |
| (l) | in the fact itself. |

## 321
## FEATHERS OR FINS

The following are birds: booby, grebe, kite, lory, moa, ousel, rail, stilt, stint, towhee, twite.
The following are fishes: bib, chub, dory, goby, gurami, keta, pope, porgy, sprod.

## 322
### OLD MASTERS

(a) Frans Hals
(b) Constable
(c) Rembrandt
(d) Vermeer
(e) Jacques-Louis David
(f) Ingres
(g) William Holman Hunt
(h) Marcel Duchamp
(i) Georges Seurat
(j) Turner.

## 323
### A ROSE BY ANY OTHER NAME

(a) Hollyhock
(b) Snapdragon
(c) Monkey Puzzle
(d) Cornflower
(e) Autumn Crocus
(f) Hawthorn
(g) Broom
(h) Candytuft
(i) Red-hot poker
(j) Sweet pea
(k) Honeysuckle
(l) Grape hyacinth
(m) Forget-me-not
(n) Catmint
(o) Poppy
(p) Virginia creeper
(q) Willow
(r) Lilac.

## 324
### SHAKESPEARE'S PEOPLE

(a) Love's Labour's Lost
(b) Antony and Cleopatra
(c) A Midsummer Night's Dream
(d) The Tempest
(e) Richard II
(f) Twelfth Night
(g) Measure For Measure
(h) The Merry Wives Of Windsor
(i) Henry IV part 2
(j) Coriolanus
(k) Macbeth
(l) Hamlet.

## 325
### COMPOSERS

(a) Tchaikovsky
(b) Elgar
(c) Vivaldi
(d) Ravel
(e) Puccini
(f) Sibelius
(g) Mozart
(h) Rossini
(i) Saint-Saëns
(j) Bizet
(k) Strauss
(l) Beethoven
(m) Verdi
(n) Rimsky-Korsakov
(o) Khatchaturian
(p) Smetana
(q) Borodin
(r) Respighi
(s) Orff
(t) Poulenc.

## 326
### WHAT'S THE YEAR?

(a) 1954
(b) 1871
(c) 1963
(d) 1920
(e) 1840
(f) 1961.

## 327
### EMINENT PEOPLE

(a) film producer
(b) landscape painter
(c) dramatist
(d) sculptor
(e) printer
(f) actor
(g) chess player
(h) architect
(i) poet
(j) educational reformer
(k) physicist
(l) pianist.

## 328
### POET'S CORNER

(a) The Owl and the Pussy-Cat went to sea (Edward Lear)
(b) I wander'd lonely as a cloud (W. Wordsworth)
(c) O what can ail thee, knight-at-arms, (John Keats)
(d) Drink to me only with thine eyes (Ben Jonson)
(e) Shall I compare thee to a summer's day? (William Shakespeare)
(f) The curfew tolls the knell of parting day (Thomas Gray)
(g) Oh, to be in England (Robert Browning)
(h) She walks in beauty like the night (Lord Byron)
(i) Hail to thee, blithe Spirit! (P. B. Shelley)
(j) And did those feet in ancient time (William Blake)
(k) Abou Ben Adhem (may his tribe increase!) (Leigh Hunt)
(l) The shades of night were falling fast (H. W. Longfellow)
(m) O say, can you see, by the dawn's early light (Francis Scott Key)
(n) Half a league, half a league, (Alfred, Lord Tennyson)
(o) Drake he's in his hammock an' a thousand mile away (Sir Henry Newbolt)
(p) I will arise and go now, and go to Innisfree (W. B. Yeats)
(q) If you can keep your head when all about you (Rudyard Kipling)
(r) If I should die, think only this of me (Rupert Brooke)
(s) I must go down to the seas again, to the lonely sea and the sky (John Masefield)
(t) 'Twas brillig, and the slithy toves (Lewis Carroll).

## 329
### QUIZ QUIZ

(a) Zloty
(b) Icosahedron
(c) Urticaria
(d) Upas
(e) Zephyrus
(f) Quincunx
(g) Ichor
(h) Utgard
(i) Quinine
(j) Zugzwang
(k) Incunabula
(l) Quetzal.

## 330
### LISTS

(a) Superior, Huron, Michigan, Erie, Ontario.
(b) Mercury, Venus, Earth, Mars, Jupiter, Saturn, Uranus, Neptune, Pluto.
(c) Aries, Taurus, Gemini, Cancer, Leo, Virgo, Libra, Scorpio, Sagittarius, Capricorn, Aquarius, Pisces.
(d) Pyramids of Egypt, Walls and hanging gardens of Babylon, Temple of Diana at Ephesus, Statue of the Olympian Zeus by Phidias, Tomb of Mausolus, Pharos of Alexandria, Colossus of Rhodes.
(e) Calliope, Clio, Erato, Euterpe, Melpomene, Polyhymnia, Terpsichore, Thalia, Urania.
(f) Anger, Covetousness, Envy, Gluttony, Lust, Pride, Sloth.
(g) Vendémiaire, Brumaire, Frimaire, Nivôse, Pluviôse, Ventôse, Germinal, Floréal, Prairial, Messidor, Thermidor (or Fervidor), Fructidor.
(h) Charles II, James II (VII of Scotland), William and Mary, Anne, George I, George II, George III, George IV, William IV, Victoria, Edward VII, George V, Edward VIII, George VI, Elizabeth II.

## 331
### JANET AND JOHN

They are both five years old.

## 332
### WHAT ARE WE?

Simply count the letters in the relevant words. Thus 'eight' contains five letters, and 'twice five' equals ten; 'ten' contains three letters, 'three' contains five, and so on.

## 333
### AN ISOSCELES TRIANGLE

An isosceles triangle has two sides the same length. The third side cannot be 7 inches (18 cm) – try drawing a triangle with sides of 15 (38), 7 (18) and 7 (18)! – so it must be 15 inches (38 cm).

## 334
### COMPLETE THE VERSE

Do not borrow from tomorrow,
Do no wrongs, know no sorrow.
Fools who only look for gold
Common comforts do not hold.

### 335
### A DRINK PROBLEM

He simply pushed the cork into the bottle.

### 336
### THE STRIKING CLOCK

At six o'clock there are five intervals between the first and last strokes. At twelve o'clock there are eleven intervals between the first and last strokes. Therefore the number of seconds taken to strike twelve will be $1\frac{1}{5}$ times 6 seconds – that is, 13.2 seconds.

### 337
### CENTIGRADE AND FAHRENHEIT

Minus 40 degrees.

### 338
### GET THE POINT?

Smith, where Jones had had 'had had', had had 'had'; 'had had' had had the examiners' approval.

### 339
### BROTHERS AND SISTERS

4 girls and 3 boys.

### 340
### A PROBLEM OF TIME

One o'clock.

### 341
### SILKWORMS

$1\frac{1}{2}$ silkworms eat $\frac{5}{2}$ leaves in $\frac{7}{2}$ minutes.
$1\frac{1}{2}$ silkworms eat 5 leaves in 7 minutes.
$1\frac{1}{2}$ silkworms eat 300 leaves in 7 hours.
$1\frac{1}{2}$ silkworms eat 7200 leaves in 7 days.
Therefore one silkworm eats 4800 leaves in one week.

### 342
### A CERTAIN NUMBER

Without any calculation, you should be able to see that twice the number is 96. Therefore the number is 48.

### 343
### A PUNCTUATION PUZZLE

That that is, is; that that is not, is not. Is not that it? It is.

### 344
### JACK AND JILL

They are two of a set of triplets (or quads, or quins, etc.).

### 345
### THE SQUARE MATHEMATICIAN

1806. When he was 43, the year was the square of his age – 1849.

### 346
### A PEACOCK PUZZLE

The whole story is a nonsense, since peacocks do not lay eggs (although *peahens* do).

### 347
### THE GARDENER'S DILEMMA

The gardener had simply to make a mound in the shape of a tetrahedron or triangular pyramid, the three sides and base being equal equilateral triangles. If he then planted one shrub at the apex and the remaining three at the angles of the base, they would be at equal distances from each other.

### 348
### ALL SIXES

95238.

### 349
### WEIGHTS

(a) Six weights are needed: 1, 2, 4, 8, 16 and 32 pounds (0.5, 1, 1.8, 3.6, 7.3, and 14.5 kilogrammes).
(b) Four weights are needed: 1, 3, 9 and 27 pounds (0.5, 1.4, 4 and 12.2 kilogrammes).

### 350
### WATCH WHERE YOU GO

Hold your watch horizontally, with the hour hand pointing in the direction of the sun. If you then visualize a line drawn halfway between the hour hand and the figure 12, that line points due south (or north if you're in the southern hemisphere). (If you happen to be wearing a *digital* watch, too bad!)

### 351
### APPLES ON A WALL

If ten the number dreamed of, why 'tis clear
That in the dream ten apples did appear.

## 352
## THE MONKEY PUZZLE

Regardless of how the monkey climbs the rope, the weight will always rise at the same rate, so that the monkey and the weight always remain opposite.

## 353
## THE KING'S WISE MEN

Five seeing, and seven blind
  Give us twelve, in all, we find;
But all of these, 'tis very plain,
  Come into account again.
For take notice, it may be true,
  That those blind of one eye are blind of two;
And consider contrariwise,
  That to see with your eye you may have your eyes;
So setting one against the other –
  For a mathematician no great bother –
And working the sum, you will understand
  That sixteen wise men still trouble the land.

## 354
## THREE SONS

15 and 18.

## 355
## A CIRCULAR RAILWAY

(a) 19   (b) The easterly traveller met 12, the other 8.

## 356
## A SPIRAL WALK

The number of yards (metres) and fractions of a yard (metre) traversed in walking along a straight piece of walk is evidently the same as the number of square yards (square metres) and fractions of a square yard (square metre) contained in that piece of walk; and the distance, traversed in passing through a square yard (square metre) at a corner is evidently a yard (metre). Hence the area of the garden is 3630 square yards (3035 square metres) – i.e. if $x$ be the width, $x(x + \frac{1}{2}) = 3630\ (3035)$. Solving the quadratic, we find $x = 60$.

Hence the dimensions are 60 yards (54.8 metres) by 60½ yards (55.3 metres).

## 357
## THE BASKET ESCAPE

(a)  The weight is sent down; the empty basket comes up.
(b)  The son goes down; the weight comes up.
(c)  The weight is taken out; the daughter goes down; the son comes up.
(d)  The son gets out; the weight goes down; empty basket comes up.
(e)  The Queen goes down; the daughter and weight come up together; the daughter gets out.
(f)  The weight goes down; empty basket comes up.
(g)  The son goes down; the weight comes up.
(h)  The daughter removes the weight and goes down; the son comes up.
(i)  The son sends down the weight; empty basket comes up.
(j)  The son goes down; the weight comes up.
(k)  The son gets out; the weight falls to the ground.

## 358
## WHAT'S THE DAY?

It was Sunday. 'When the day after tomorrow (Tuesday) is yesterday, today (Wednesday) will be as far from Sunday as today (Thursday) was from Sunday when the day before yesterday (Friday) was tomorrow.' From Thursday to Sunday is three days, as is also from Sunday to Wednesday.

## 359
## TWELVE ROWS

The men arranged themselves in the form of a regular dodecagon, with the officer at the centre.

## 360
## NOT SO LOYAL?

Read the first line of the first verse, then the first line of the second verse; next the second line of the first verse, then the second line of the second verse, and so on.

## 361
## TRUE OR BLUFF

(a) True
(b) True
(c) Bluff – conjee is water in which rice has been boiled
(d) True
(e) Bluff – a pygostyle is the bone of a bird's tail
(f) Bluff – a cavesson is a nose-band for a horse
(g) True
(h) Bluff – a dicynodont is an extinct tusked reptile
(i) True
(j) True.

## 362
## A VIEW OF THE EARTH

At a distance equal to the diameter of the earth – approximately 7900 miles.

## 363
## THE ANAGRAM PROGRAM

The answers are:

(a) 119
(b) 359
(c) 1259
(d) 839
(e) 90,719
(f) 415,799.

The valid anagrams (words that may be found in a dictionary) are:

(a) arets, aster, astre, earst, rates, reast, resat, strae, tares, tears, teras
(b) arrect, carter, tracer
(c) caterer, retrace
(d) sleeted, steeled
(e) dissenter, tiredness
(f) there aren't any that I know of.

## 364
## THE END OF THE WORLD

The first day of a century can never fall on a Sunday (nor on a Wednesday nor a Friday)!

## 365
## COMMANDOS

Multiply the mile distance (5280 feet) by the height (300 feet) and you get 1,584,000. Add 5280 feet to twice the height (600 feet) and you get 5880. Divide the former result by the latter – and $269\frac{19}{49}$ feet is the required answer.